Time for the UK to Face the Facts

What the politicians do not want to admit and why they do not tell

by

CHRISTOPHER HOSKIN

The June Press

First published in 2013

by The June Press Ltd

UK distributor
The June Press Ltd
PO Box 119
Totnes
Devon TQ9 7WA
Tel: 44(0)8456 120 175
Email: info@junepress.com
Web: www.junepress.com

ISBN 978-0-9534697-9-6

The Author

Christopher Hoskin, has a degree in philosophy from Cambridge and a mathematical model which he designed is on display at the Science Museum in London.

He has closely followed British history and the European debate for many years, publishing a number of publications on Britain and its relationship with the EU.

In this book he looks in depth, at the problems created by our political leaders lack of understanding of the real world, and how that impinges on the public it is supposed to represent.

Acknowledgements

I wish to express my deepest gratitude to the many people who helped in the production of this book. My special thanks go to Professor Stephen F. Bush and Derek Norman.

Christopher Hoskin, 2013

Contents

Introduction

In my previous publications I have discussed Britain's membership of the EU, immigration, overseas aid, the controversy about man-made global warming and the maintenance of Britain as one country. In this new book I continue to point out the importance of these questions, but I also consider the takeovers of much of British industry by foreign concerns and the mistaken belief that the economy can be sustained by financial services alone.

The unfortunate situation in which Britain is placed today is the result of an unholy combination of harmful influences from both the right and left. From the right are the machinations of people who are sufficiently rich and privileged that they are unaffected by ills which trouble the rest of us, who only consider short term advantage and who only think in narrow economic terms. From the left are the machinations of fanatical devotees of political correctness and multiculturalism, who dislike the heritage of this country. Both sets of people have shown a lack of patriotism and common sense which contrasts greatly with their forebears.

The issues I discuss in this book are in my view more important than the common concerns of ordinary party politics. They involve the totally unnecessary expenditure of vast sums of money which could be better spent on other things. At a time of financial stringency this waste is particularly galling, but of still more importance, if the ills which I have described are allowed to continue, this country is at risk of becoming a totally different place to what it was in the past and to what people assume it to be today. The cause of the trouble is that we are governed by an elite on all sides of politics whose needs and desires are remote from the people they aspire to represent.

1

Political and Economic Background

Economics not of sole importance

Many people both on the left and right think that the economic aspect of things is the only thing that matters. This is not so. There is an economic aspect of a person's life, but that person has a life which cannot be described in economic terms. There is an economic aspect of the history of a nation, but that nation has a history which cannot be so described either.

Nigel Lawson in his book "*The View From No 11*" expounds an economic view of events. There is nothing wrong with that but it is just one of many views. He suggests that the treasury should dominate the government as opposed to the spending departments. Certainly we do not want to spend money unnecessarily but we need to know what the money is spent on as well as how much money is spent. There are some things on which money should be spent and other things on which it should not. There are some projects which should be given the go ahead and be financed and other projects which should not. Ultimately the money to be spent has to come from the taxpayer but there are some things that we should strongly advise the taxpayer to support and other things which we should definitely not.

Before we discuss finance, we should ask ourselves what we actually want and what we don't want. We should ask ourselves questions about the value of things. Then and only then can we discuss the cost of things. We need to have a very firm grasp of the subject matter that we are dealing with and of the various alternative remedies which are on offer, before we consider the costs. When we do consider them, we should not just choose the cheapest alternative, but the alternative which gives us what we want. We should be prepared to pay to have the job done properly. This may seem profligate but there are plenty of unnecessary items on which we can economise to compensate us for spending more on what is worthwhile.

A person who concentrates solely on the economic aspect of things is like somebody who concentrates solely on the means of transport to a place of entertainment while ignoring what the entertainment is all about.

The succeeding chapters will deal with constraints on our national life which no serious politician can ignore. If they pretend that these do not exist they will be conducting the economic policy of this country with one arm tied behind their backs. We need to first get the political priorities right. If we do this we will be gratified by how much money we shall save and by how much easier it makes our decisions about the economy.

British industry compared with that of Germany

Britain was the first country to have an industrial revolution. For a time she was the workshop of the world, but her predominance began to be challenged from about 1850. Her share of world trade fell by over 10% between 1870 and 1914, with Germany already the major competitor. This pattern of Germany doing better than Britain in respect of industrial performance has continued, despite the interruptions of two world wars, right through to the present day.

The countries which followed Britain in industrialising had an advantage in that they could start at a more advanced level. Further, unlike her competitors, Britain, by virtue of her empire and the availability of abundant supplies of cheap labour and raw materials, had little incentive to improve its productivity and modernise. By 1914 Britain was still dominant in the coal and cotton industries, but Germany led in the newer sectors of steel, machinery and chemicals. Germany had 650 trained chemical engineers whereas Britain only had 40. Britain in the early 19th century had led the world with the steam engine, but Germany at its end was leading in advanced technology.

Around 50% of the growth of the German economy during the twenty years following the 2nd World War was probably due to technological advances, whereas during the same period British manufacturing was characterised by outdated plant and reluctance to move quickly into new technological areas. Britain's education system was developed in the 19th century to serve the needs of its empire and emphasised administrative and cultural skills, and it did not sufficiently re-orientate itself after the loss of the empire. In contrast Germany strongly promoted skills in science and technology. The fashionable elite of Britain looked down on engineering. In Germany engineers are more respected and are ranked on a par with doctors and lawyers. German firms were much more keen to use regular training of apprentices to make up their skilled labour force, whereas British firms tended just to recruit on the labour market. Furthermore, the German tradition is for a considerable involvement of banks in industry. German banks will lend up to two thirds of asset value if they believe in a company, whereas in Britain it is often difficult for smaller firms to get more than one third. There are in Germany often long standing personal relationships between company executives and bank managers. In addition the Allied occupation of West Germany gave her a small number of industry based trades unions, which was the opposite of the situation in Britain and which reduced to a minimum the incidence of demarcation and inter-union disputes.

This became the norm all over Germany when it was reunited.

In addition financing of investments tends to be long-term in Germany, whereas the pressure exerted by the City of

London in Britain leads to much shorter investment horizons, which eventually determine conventional management attitudes.

There were burdens which Britain suffered from in the years after the 2nd World War which were not suffered by West Germany. Britain was in debt to the United States and still possessed overseas territories - not yet independent - for which she was responsible. Britain had considerable military commitments and was the centre of the Sterling Area, which limited her freedom to devalue the pound. She had also decided right from the start of this period to have a fully fledged welfare state. All this meant that she could not devote sufficient resources to modernising her industry as would have been desirable.

Industrial disputes were much more part of the scene in Britain than in West Germany during the first few decades after the war. Particularly damaging were demarcation disputes which the multiplicity of unions in British industry favoured.

The failure to exploit British inventions was another unfortunate thing about Britain in the 20th century. Frank Whittle invented the jet engine well before the 2nd World War. If he had been given full backing from the beginning, it would have been a great help in the war. The hovercraft was another British invention which we did not exploit to the full and even the harrier jump-jet was not seen for its full potential until the Falklands war.

Capitalism and communism

I make serious criticisms of developments in Britain in the last thirty years, but I am and always have been totally opposed to communism. In the battle between the West and the communist East, my allegiance has always been totally to the West.

Communism is associated with the totalitarian regimes of the Communist states, with the slave labour camps, with the massacres and with all the various atrocities for which they were responsible. Casting this aside for the moment, let us have a look at what were supposedly the ideals of communism.

Communism arose from a hostility to the ills of the industrial capitalism of the 19th century. A natural reaction to those ills would be to try and mitigate them by a whole series of controls, limiting the hours and conditions of work and giving greater security to the workers in sickness and unemployment. All these things have in fact been done, but this has never satisfied true communists. According to them the capitalist system itself is irredeemable and cannot be rectified.

In its Marxist form, communism owes its worldwide influence to the fact that it was adopted as the official ideology of Russia and China, which were and are large and powerful countries. It would not have had the same influence if it had only been adopted by a small country like Albania.

Marxist Communism claimed to be scientific, which it certainly is not. It enhanced its credentials in the minds of the credulous by latching on to the prestige of science. It believed in a self selected class of people who make decisions about all matters both political and economic allegedly on behalf of the general population, in a manner miraculously detached from any form of self interest. Moreover, it also believed in the supposed magic of collective activity as opposed to individual action.

Advocates of a free economy remember that the vast majority of goods and services in the modern world were originally invented or created by private individuals, not by politicians, government ministers or political activists. If anything new is invented or created tomorrow, it too will owe its creation to a private individual. Even where something is run as a public corporation, there is, to put it poetically, a private core inside the nationalised industry. Where this is lacking or weak the enterprise is diminished in quality.

We in the West believed and still do believe in a free economy and a democratic politics with opposing parties and we are devoted to the rights of the individual. At least that is the theory. In practice there were and are bureaucratic individuals and would-be despots in both systems. As the Russian dissident, Vladimir Bukovsky, said at the end of his book, "*To Build A Castle*", "Those who think that the frontier between freedom and un-freedom corresponds with the State frontiers of the Soviet Union are cruelly mistaken".

Nevertheless the Cold War between the West and the Communist block was a real conflict, with real differences between the opposing systems. In my opinion any person who aspired to real intelligence and real goodwill towards mankind would have said of Communism that he or she was against it.

There is the case of China which has emerged from its Maoist period to a new period of greater liberality and ever increasing wealth. I do not know whether China will eventually take the Western democratic path. If it does it will only be after many decades or even centuries. The fact is that China and Japan have always been alien to the civilisation of the West, and continue to be so today.

Communism has influenced people even when they are avowed democrats and opposed to the totalitarian communist regimes. As a political philosophy it is either fraudulent or the product of wishful thinking, or possibly a bit of both. It must be distinguished from a desire to improve the lot of one's fellow human beings, which is a totally different phenomenon.

Sometimes people who have been influenced by communism will not offer constructive criticism of the workings of a capitalist economy, because they do not believe in it. Now that the old Soviet Union has collapsed and communism has been discredited, some people may look upon everything capitalist with favour. So there are two groups of people who will refrain from constructive criticism of the workings of our economy.

Consideration of Mrs Thatcher

Mrs Thatcher had things to her credit as well as things to her discredit.

She was right to stand four square with Ronald Reagan against the evil empire of the old Soviet Union, and right too to welcome the new look from Russia in the shape of Mikhael Gorbachov. She instinctively understood the main global conflict of her time and she understood the nuclear deterrent as her unilateralist opponents did not.

Mrs Thatcher was right to decide to send the task force to re-take the Falkland Islands after they had been invaded by Argentina. She understood that what was involved was something, much more important than the Falklands themselves, it was the determination of Britain to defend herself when attacked and the self esteem of the British people. However, she and her government must also accept the blame for planning to cut down on the navy prior to the invasion and for withdrawing the one ship which was in the area at the time. This sent the wrong signal to the Argentines, who thought that the British government would do nothing if they invaded. Mrs Thatcher, like many of our politicians, failed to recognise the connection between having a particular policy and possessing the means to carry it out.

She and Norman Tebbit were right to enact their trades union reforms. In fact they could have been made stronger if the required secret ballot of members before a strike had been a secret ballot of all the members, not just of those who were present. The resistance to these measures was expected but the government were in the right. This part of their industrial policy was correct because the country had been bedevilled by official and unofficial strikes particularly in the seventies, but off and on since the war.

The sale of council houses was popular, but it did involve some people in house ownership who could not afford it. Unfortunately there was no obligation on councils to use the money from the sale to build more council houses.

In contrast to the above there are issues, on which she is claimed by some to have displayed wisdom, where, with hindsight her record was not so good.

Before she became leader of the Conservative Party Mrs Thatcher was distinctly in favour of the EU. In the 1975 referendum she was one of the leaders of the Conservative section of the pro EU campaign. It was only after she had been prime minister for a few years that she decided that our contribution to the EU budget was too much and she fought for it to be reduced. In return for our EU partners agreeing to accept this, she signed the Single European Act, thus doing away with Britain's veto on a number of matters. At the end of her premiership in a speech she made in Bruges, she expressed doubts about the way the EU was moving towards a federal state. Her euroscepticism was late in the day and failed to foresee the problems of the future until they were at the front door.

There was the issue of the preservation of the grammer schools. The latter had been one of the greatest instruments for social mobility during the period of their existence. It might be thought that a conservative would fight to preserve them and in the process gain much popular support. In practice during her time as Education Secretary and during her premiership she did nothing to prevent their being supplanted by comprehensive schools. The result has been to the detriment of both education and of social mobility.

The Poll Tax was a mistake and launching it first in Scotland was a further mistake. At this point in time it was essential to avoid any measure which could endanger the maintenance of Great Britain as one country. This did not seem to occur to her or to any of her ministers. Further, although theoretically it would be nice if all recipients could contribute to the services of which they are the beneficiaries, in fact many of them cannot do so and the old rates were the most practical way of financing local government. The old rates were fair in the sense that the larger and more valuable your property the more you paid.

Thatcher's ecomic policy

In considering the monetarist policy of Mrs Thatcher and her government, we should realise that her lieutenants, such as Howe and Heseltine, who were later to come out against her, bear as great a responsibility for it as she did.

The purpose of the monetarist policy was to reduce inflation and in this it succeeded. Unfortunately a great number of British manufacturing companies went to the wall in this period together with the jobs which they provided. That may not have been the intention, but it happened. During her premiership North Sea oil had come on the scene. The Thatcher government could have used the revenues from this to help British industry. Instead these revenues were used to prop up the value of the pound, thus making exporting more difficult for British companies. The government's policies on the value of the currency, interest rates and VAT were very burdensome on British companies and were too much for many of them. Further this fate overtook companies whether they were successful or not. It was not discriminatory. The inescapable conclusion was that the government did not care.

While the Thatcher government were keen to attract foreign firms to set up plants in Britain, it seemed to care little for British manufacturing industry. As an example of the government's attitude to foreign firms, Nissan received £35 million in selective assistance and another £90 million in regional grants (more than one third of the plant's cost) to set up in the North East. Some people, with long memories of their treatment of our prisoners of war in the 2nd World War, were perhaps not so keen on such a welcome being given to the Japanese, but the Thatcher government were only sensitive to economic considerations. We may ask why, if the Thatcher government was willing to do this, it was not willing to assist appropriate British companies. It almost seems as if the government had a prejudice against British management. I am quite sure that if you looked hard enough you would have found British managers quite as capable as those from overseas. I remember at the time watching the television and hearing a businessman say that Mrs Thatcher backed his competitors. Nigel Lawson made the remark that the future was in service industries. The government became very enamoured with finance, deregulating the City of London and hoping that it could be the main support of the economy.

Furthermore, although Mrs Thatcher's victory over Arthur Scargill in the Miners Strike was desirable and necessary, the government did not attempt to sweeten the pill when the strike was over. She should never have made those comments about the miners that they were the enemy within. Whatever she thought of Scargill and his militants, the vast majority of the miners were her fellow citizens and she should have acknowledged them as such. It is not surprising that great parts of the country did not like Thatcherism.

In considering Mrs Thatcher, we must realise that her mind set was almost solely concerned with the economic aspect of things. Even her opposition to communism was much tainted with this. She criticised the Russians for neglecting the market. Thatcher thought above all about the balance of payments and the battle against inflation. She was not really interested in who owned British industry and equated freedom with economic freedom. She saw her fellow countrymen as potentially successful grocers like her father.

My mother, whose father was a Glasgow merchant at the beginning of the 20th century, said that Mrs Thatcher did not understand heavy industry. She had a degree in chemistry and worked as a research chemist for BX Plastics in Colchester and then at Allied Lyons in London for a short time, but I don't think it made her at home with the world of industry and its problems.

Michael Portillo, who was a minister in her government, left politics and went into the media. He did a very good series of railway journeys about Britain for television, stopping at local industries on the way. Later, he said that he wished that he had made these journeys before going into politics rather than after. Most politicians of all parties could benefit by doing this. Politicians seem to be concerned about industry, only if something goes wrong such as a damaging strike, or if there is a closure of a factory in their constituency with the accompanying loss of jobs. They seem only to be concerned about industry if there is a party political advantage to gained from it.

The CBI spent the Thatcher decade, between restatements of support for the Conservatives at election times, warring with the government about the effects of its policies on manufacturing industry. Quite frankly one wonders why it did not sponsor a party dedicated to supporting British industry in opposition to them. The true origin of the Conservatives being labelled as the nasty party is not the scepticism of most Conservatives about the current trendy pseudo-left agenda, but the downgrading of British industry, those who worked in it and the excessive reliance on the world of finance.

The City of London

The financial services of the City of London are a definite contributor to the British economy. How much may be a matter of dispute, but it is definitely significant. Therefore, it is totally against the national interest to allow the EU to interfere in the affairs of the City in any way. However, total reliance on financial services is a very serious mistake. In 2005 financial services with around 1.1 million employees in many centres across the country made a net contribution to our foreign earnings of only about twice that of our pharmaceutical industry, which employs under 200,000 people.

Recently the general consensus is that the financial sector has got out of hand. It has been suggested that regulations of one kind or another are needed. Some say that the regulations would not achieve the desired effect. It is difficult for the lay person to form a proper judgement on the matter, since economists have their own technical language, which none of them seem willing or able to translate into terms intelligible to laymen. Like all professionals, it is an advantage to express themselves thus, so that any interference by laymen in their affairs can be avoided.

My main concern is to put a stop to the predatory takeovers of British public companies and utilities by foreigners, which has occurred so much in recent years. This has been made possible by the financial sector lending the required sums of money to predators for them to accomplish the takeovers by the use of unsecured debt. In the section on "Prospects for British industry" I advocate legislating to do something about this. I also advocate a much greater cooperation of local banks with British firms large or small.

Apart from the above suggestions I have nothing to say about the financial sector, because I do not know enough about it. However, I would suggest that avoidance of unsecured debt is a good principle, which they should abide by unless they have very good reasons. Another aspect of finance in recent years which seems odd is that top bankers appear to get just as much remuneration when things go wrong as when they go right. I always thought that under capitalism you were rewarded for success and punished for failure.

Rich foreigners in Britain

There are rich foreigners owning property in Britain, overseas students at British universities and people from overseas employed in the social services such as the NHS.

Rich foreigners have always been allowed to own property in Britain and in the last fifty years increasing numbers of them have chosen to do so. At the time before the advent of the council tax local government was financed by rates on the value of the property people owned, those owning large and expensive properties paid proportionally high rates. Today that is no longer the case. A good proportion of rich foreigners reside here for only a part of the year and do not pay British income tax and they pay relatively modest amounts of council tax. While they are here they spend money and therefore benefit the country in that way. They may make extensive alterations to their properties, which benefits the firms they employ to do this. On the minus side their acquisition of property in Britain tends to put house prices up. We may ask whether this is to the benefit of this country.

There has been quite a lot of buying up of property in Britain by foreigners for investment purposes, both in a small way and in a big way. Now ownership and control go together and there may be cause for concern. Sometimes this may result in altering the character of a neighbourhood. We may ask what is the effect of large properties being owned by people whose interests are not necessarily the same as those of the British people.

A good proportion of overseas students study at British universities. All of them pay considerably more for their studies than British students, even with tuition fees at their present level. This obviously helps the universities financially. Without it either the government or private donors would have to step in. Furthermore, the overseas students spend money while they are here. However, this could mean that there are fewer university places for British students. Also not all of the overseas students return home after their studies end, but stay on here illegally.

There is today the practice of hiring personnel from overseas to staff our social services such as the NHS. This has been going on for quite some time. It is a cheaper alternative to training our own people. This is short term penny pinching. We should really be training our own people and we should not begrudge the expense of doing so.

2

The Fate of British Industry

Foreign takeovers of British firms

In this section I am heavily indebted to the book "*Britain For Sale*" by Alex Brummer.

The foreign takeover of a British company which really hit the headlines was the takeover of Cadbury by the American firm Kraft in 2009. It became newsworthy because Cadbury was a household name in Britain as a maker of chocolate. It had been there since the 1850s and its philanthropic owners had built the world famous village of Bournville for their employees. In spite of this it was not a firm whose existence in British hands was strategically necessary for the country. Afterwards the Cadbury Somerdale plant at Keynsham near Bristol was closed in 2010 in spite of a promise at the time of the takeover to keep it open.

In 2011 Kraft gave notice that a further 150 posts would go at Cadbury's historic Bournville factory in 2012. This was a familiar feature of foreign takeovers.

Another case was the takeover of the high street chain Alliance Boots by the Italian pharmacy king Stephano Pessina and private equity barons KKR in 2007 for £12 billion. Soon after the takeover, Boots, based in Nottingham for 161 years, moved its headquarters to Zug in Switzerland. Before the takeover Boots paid £89 million in tax in Britain in its final year as a quoted company on the stock market. Now that it pays its tax in Zug that figure has shrunk to just £9 million.

There were other takeovers of far greater importance which did not elicit such concern. An example was ICI. In the spring of 2007 speculation about the company was rife in expectation of a bid from someone. The board of ICI had been working out how much they thought the company was worth. If the buyer made an offer below what they had in mind they would be shown the door, but if they offered the stated value or above they would be obliged, acting for the shareholders, to take it seriously. Before going any further, the chairman of ICI did ask whether anyone in the government or in the upper reaches of Whitehall had any kind of policy about protecting British companies. The answer was that they did not think it was part of the government's job to protect ICI or anyone else from a foreign takeover. They said that they were interested in jobs, but not in who owns a company.

On 6th August 2007, the buyer, AkzoNobel, raised its offer to 670 pence per ICI share or £8 billion. The deal was finally completed on 2nd January 2008 after AkzoNobel had agreed to sell its Manchester-based Crown Paints subsidiary to satisfy the EU Competition Commissioner.

Let us take a brief look at what sort of company ICI was. It was a company which offered thousands of different products, ranging from pharmaceutical to paints to agrochemicals. It led the way in the commercial exploitation of polyurethanes (which alongside plastics and polythene had been developed in the ICI laboratories) into such products as cavity insulation for walls, refrigeration on ships and durable soles for shoes. It became the biggest manufacturer of pain combatting drugs. In spite of some minor problems ICI, with its focus on speciality chemicals, dyestuffs and paints, was continuing to battle strongly for Britain in overseas markets. Its research and development laboratories were still going strong. The fate of ICI was determined not because it was a company on the ropes looking for a saviour, far from it. What made it vulnerable was an official lack of interest in what might happen to it and a focus on share price to the exclusion of other considerations.

After the takeover, 29 factories including several in Britain were closed. As of 2011, some research and development was still in Britain. There are research laboratories in Slough and Newcastle, but there is no guarantee that all or any of these will remain, particularly if AkzoNobel sells off further parts of the company.

Another tragic loss of a British company was Pilkington, the glass manufacturers and pioneer of the technique of float glass to produce sheets of uniform thickness and flatness, ideal for architectural work. It prospered as an independent company and became a major global player. The Japanese rival Nippon Glass offered £2.2 billion in 2006 and a reluctant board capitulated. Pilkington was doing perfectly well and it suffered a takeover for the same reasons as ICI.

With the sale of GEC's share of train manufacture to the French firm Alstom, after the breakup of Lord Weinstock's empire in the early 1990s, British train production was run down and transferred to France. Local train manufacturing became a shadow of its former self. How far things had declined emerged when the Conservative led coalition government decided in June 2011 to award a £3 billion contract for new rolling stock for the Thameslink line to the German manufacturer Siemens, instead of to Bombardier, which was Britain's last domestically centred train maker.

In the same way in 2001 Westland, Britain's last helicopter maker was merged with Italy's Finmeccanica helicopter division. When the deal was done the newly named AugustaWestland began shedding staff in Britain with 1,000 jobs going. This was evidently cheaper and easier than laying off staff in Italy. Since then much of the core research and development and design has been shifted to Italy, leaving Yeovil, where Westland had been based, as an assembly plant.

In 2011 there was the £7.1 billion takeover by the American company Hewlett Packard of the British software group Autonomy, founded in 1996, which was a market leader using technologies arising from Cambridge University research. That is not a triumph for Silicon Fen, Cambridge's high-tech park, as some have claimed, but a potential nail in the coffin of British software expertise. After all Hewlett Packard was doing what it did in order to gain skills it did not have but needed.

In 2007, Corus, the core of which was the old British Steel, was bought by the Indian conglomerate Tata. As the recession started to bite in 2009, Tata moved to slim down its operations. Of 3,500 jobs axed worldwide, some 2,500 were cut in Britain, mostly in depressed regions hugely reliant on heavy industry.

The history of the British car industry has been troublesome. Nevertheless it is interesting that some 10,000 Minis are produced by their new owner BMW at their new factory in Oxford. The Mini, which was a good and popular car, was judged rightly by its German owners to be worth manufacturing. Of course a far-sighted British owner might have been able to do the same.

Demarcation disputes before Thatcher

Before Mrs Thatcher's period in office industrial disputes were part of the landscape of Britain. Some were about pay, but the most damaging were either objecting to the introduction of more modern machinery or about who should operate it. Examples of industries where the above type of problems occurred were shipbuilding, cars, textiles and coal.

It is inevitable that, as time passes, new more modern machinery will displace the old machines and that new more efficient ways of doing things will replace the old ways. This process will mean that fewer personnel will be required than in the past. If this is not allowed to happen, the alternatives are:

(1) Continuation with the old machinery and the existing number of workers. This option will probably result in the firm ceasing to be competitive and thus going out of business.

(2) Dismissal of the old workforce and hire of immigrants

whom you can pay less. In the 1950s some textile firms in the North did just that, hiring new workers from the Indian subcontinent instead of modernising. This just postponed the day of the firm's closure.

Unsurprisingly the workforce and the unions were not too happy about the above economic reality. The management of some companies put off modernising for fear of offending the latter. Before Mrs Thatcher, postwar governments were continually pumping money into companies to postpone the evil day and please the constituencies of the areas where the workforce resided.

Mrs Thatcher followed a policy of not helping companies in trouble if she could avoid it. She thought firms should be left to sink or swim without interference. So British companies, which were in trouble but had potential and which could have been rescued by judicious injection of funds, were allowed to go out of business. She also ran the economy to obtain low inflation with scant regard to the needs of industry. If the unions were partly responsible for the non-competitiveness of much of British industry, they were punished not by their desires being rejected but by their companies going to the wall.

The blame for the collapse of much of British industry must lie with three protagonists: the unions, the management and the government.

The culpability of successive governments lie with their lack of interest or enthusiasm for British industry except in so far as narrow political concerns were involved. They failed to link the value of the pound to the effect it had on companies trying to export. Certain sectors of industry were hindered by the political battle between nationalisation and denationalisation. Interest rates and taxation generally were often decided on because of the likely effects on consumers rather than because of their effects on industry. When the government intervened to promote mergers it was not always beneficial for industry.

The policy of persuading companies to relocate parts of their plant to distressed areas was often damaging to companies economically.

Some unions and elements of the workforce in some companies showed little understanding of the necessity of firms to be viable and acted as if economic realities did not exist. There was definitely a small but significant minority of politically motivated union men who used industrial disputes for ideological purposes. In the years before the Tebbit reforms - instituting a secret ballot - it was easy for these men to have their way. It is important to realise that strikes and industrial disputes were very costly to companies, with lost production being just one of the more obvious costs. Union action preventing necessary modernisations was also extremely costly and damaging to a firm's survival.

Some managements did not see the need to change anyway. They trusted in the old ways and the old products. There was often a lack of awareness of what competitors in other countries were doing. Often there was a tendency to rely on the successes of past performance and a reluctance to innovate partly from a fear of the likely disruption it could cause. Just as there were undoubtedly cases of good management, where the management had a good relationship with the workforce, so there were certainly cases of bad management, where the reverse was the case.

By the time that Mrs Thatcher came upon the scene, much of British industry appeared uncompetitive internationally and there was an atmosphere of despair in the minds of politicians when they thought about it. They did not know what to do to improve matters and they failed to recognise their own contribution to the plight in which it found itself. That explains the attitudes of the Thatcher government, though it certainly does not excuse them.

Modernisation should have been encouraged to go ahead and the true role of the government should have been to help financially all British companies, which were prepared to cooperate, to accomplish this and to survive without being subject to takeovers by foreigners. There was a need to sweeten the pill for the displaced workforce, with redundancy money, early retirement and retraining. The training of new personnel and retraining of old personnel, with an emphasis on flexibility to meet the different tasks to be fulfilled was essential. The true role of the government should have been the giving of grants to firms to make this possible and to compensate those workers for whom retraining was not possible. Pretending to super-manage companies in trouble was not helpful.

The mining industry presented particular problems. Where unprofitable mines were closed down (assuming that they were in fact unprofitable), there were dire effects on entire communities and the self respect of the unemployed miners was an issue which needed full consideration. These ex-miners often felt that previously they had been employed to do a real job, whereas, after being made redundant, they were either unemployed or doing jobs for which they did not feel the same about at all. The problems of some other parts of heavy industry were similar.

The government, the unions and the management were all responsible for the decline of British industry but the common thread running through the actions of almost everybody, including the general public, was the lack of the will and determination to prevent the decline and enable it to prosper.

Dangers of foreign ownership of British utilities

An extreme example of this is given by the residential health provider Southern Cross. The American firm Blackstone saw a commercial opportunity in buying up and stitching together privately run care homes across Britain. It created a single entity which could source services centrally and provide a common standard of care. However, Blackstone was not prepared to be a long-term owner, but saw an opportunity to make a quick profit by floating Southern Cross as a public company, on the London stock market. In the process it collected £600 million of profits, but the company it created was badly equipped to cope with the economic downturn that began with the 2007-2009 financial crisis. In the following years a combination of lack of investment, poor management and rising rents charged by landlords brought Southern Cross to the brink, placing its 750 homes and 31,000 elderly residents at serious risk by the middle of 2011. In June 2011 the shares of the company were suspended on the stock market and Southern Cross unilaterally cut the rents it paid to landlords by 30%. It also announced that it would be cutting 3,000 jobs out of its workforce of 44,000 (this would raise questions about quality of care). In July 2011, 249 of the 752 homes were rescued when landlord NHP reached a deal with Court Cavendish, another health care group. Another 250 were taken back into ownership by the landlords who agreed to operate the homes. The fate of the rest of the homes remained unsettled.

Utility companies with an international reach can easily transfer profits from one part of the world to another, rather than reinvest them in infrastructure, service and lower prices in the host country. In 2011 it was disclosed that Iberdrola, the Spanish owners of Scottish Power, used a cash surplus at its Scottish Power subsidiary to make a ten-year loan of £800 million to its sister company in the United States. There was immediate controversy in Scotland, which has seen an average rise of 40% in energy bills since 2007. In contrast Iberdrola's American customers have had their gas and electricity bills frozen since the mid-1990s until the imposition of a 4% to 8% rise in 2011.

Another interesting story was that of Thames Water. The latter had 8.5 million water customers and 13.5 million waste water clients. It operated 100 water treatment plants, 290 pumping stations and 235 reservoirs. In 2001, a decade after privatisation, it was snapped up by the German company RWE. By 2005 profits had climbed 30% to £346 million with the help of a 21% price rise imposed on its customers. The jump in earnings was achieved despite a failure to develop or fix the ancient infrastructure. By 2005 its pipe infrastructure in Britain leaked a disgraceful 196 million gallons a day. During the succeeding summer of 2006, there was a serious drought and water rationing was introduced. *The Daily Mail* ran a series of articles on what it regarded as the uncaring attitude of Thames Water's absentee owners. It revealed the staggering salaries of these people and that in Laren in Holland, where one of them lived, the water supplies were plentiful and there was no trouble. Yet, while the average Thames Water customer was paying £265 a year, Laren residents paid well under half that amount for a first-class modern supply network.

Some people would remark that British firms have themselves invested elsewhere and particularly in the United States. However, the reality of such cases is interesting. A British firm, National Grid, invested in New York state and the Eastern Seaboard, but they found that pricing and investment decisions are strictly policed by state and city authorities. Also, that prices cannot be raised by company dictate. Any proposed price increase is subjected to public hearings, in which all interested groups have their say. The states demand full disclosure of internal financial information including details of the costs and lifestyles of executives. Although in theory America welcomes foreign buyers, in practice many of the states place such firm controls on intruders that these effectively act as a deterrent to overseas involvement. In Britain we have overseas ownership and no real accountability.

By 2010 just 34% of the fuel for the British economy remained in British hands. 32% was under French control, 27% was in the hands of German enterprises and 7% was under Spanish control. A concern of Alistair Buchanan, who became head of the energy regulator Ofgem, was that foreign-owned utilities have a record of instantly passing on price increases to British consumers when oil and gas prices are rising, but failing to adjust them downwards fast enough, if at all, when wholesale prices are falling. Another danger is this. If another energy crisis were to occur on the scale of that of the 1970s, Britain would be in real trouble. The big continental energy firms such as RWE and E.ON would naturally feel more of an obligation to keep the Ruhr supplied rather than Tyneside or other parts of Britain, if they had to choose. In the Arctic winter of 2010-2011, the gas supplies through the Langeled Britain-Norway pipeline were substantially reduced, because the Norwegians understandably prioritised themselves and their closest trading partners.

Foreign ownership in the transport area

In 1991 Britain's biggest container port Felixstowe was bought by the Hong Kong based trading empire Hutchinson Whampoa. Since then it has enjoyed large inward investment by its new owners, but the considerable income and profits that have flowed in have been repatriated overseas. Instead of being an international hub for Britain, it has effectively become an outpost of Hong Kong.

Associated British Ports (which began life as the British Transport Docks Board and which was privatised by the Thatcher government in 1982) handled a quarter of Britain's seaborne trade from 21 ports, including Southampton, Plymouth, Cardiff and Immingham. In July 2006 the regulators cleared a foreign consortium £3.17 billion takeover bid. ABP is now controlled from Jersey, which is outside British tax jurisdiction.

In March 2011 Forth Ports, which had control of London's Tilbury Docks, several Scottish ports and 400 acres of Edinburgh waterfront, was sold for £754 million to an assortment of financial groups led by a little-known European firm.

The Peninsular and Oriental Steam Navigation Company was founded about 170 years ago and had an unparalleled international infrastructure of container ports and ships. It built up a network of ports across the Pacific and the Middle East to add to those it already controlled in Britain and the United States. As trade rose, so did freight rates and the opportunity for logistical, insurance and financial deals. The company was bought in March 2006 by Dubai Ports World for £6.8 billion. As a result of this short-sightedness by the get rich quick merchants in the City of London, Britain no longer has a presence in a market that it once dominated. Imports and exports pass through our ports. Income is generated by container and terminal handling fees, shipping agencies, dredging, marine consultancy and also financial services such as insurance. All that has passed beyond national control.

At a time when other maritime nations, such as China and the United Arab Emirates, are jealously guarding their own trading hubs and snapping up ports across the world, Britain has willingly sold off a great chunk of the nation's infrastructure to the highest bidder, without any thought for the long-term affect of it.

Arriva was a British company that thrived in the environment created by privatisation. Originally a bus company, it came to run a large number of Britain's big city networks, including 20% of London's routes. It also expanded into mainland Europe, to such an extent that by 2010, 42% of Arriva's profits and revenues were earned there. In April 2010 the German railway company Deutsche Bahn bought it for £1.5 billion. The government chose not to intervene. Ray Massey of *The Daily Mail* lamented the loss of yet another key element of Britain's manufacturing and infrastructure to foreign ownership.

The British Airports Authority (BAA), which had been

privatised by the Thatcher government, was sold in June 2006 to the Spanish construction company Ferrovial for £10.6 billion. Later it was forced to sell off Gatwick, Stanstead and one of the Scottish airports to buyers, who were also foreign, in order to comply with the rulings of the Competition Commission. Ferrovial had no experience of running anything on the scale of one of Europe's biggest hub airports. In addition it was, after its acquisition, saddled with debt. Even though BAA's running of the airports had not attracted much praise, Ferrovial's running of them was even worse. While the latter was hoping to run the business for cash, the airports in fact badly needed investment. London's airports groaned under the weight of passenger numbers. Overcrowding became part of the experience of flying. Heathrow Terminal 5 came late and had teething troubles.

There has been an occasion when a foreign owner of a British enterprise was punished for its failure to run it in the best interests of its customers. Connex, the French owners of the former British Rail Southern Region performed unsatisfactorily when they had control of one of Britain's busiest commuter networks. Punctuality was bad and the promised investment in new rolling stock never took place. The franchise, awarded in 1996, had originally been intended to run until 2011. But in June 2003 the Strategic Rail Authority cut short the franchise, citing poor financial management and "serious loss of confidence in the ability of the company to run the business in the widest sense".

The history of British ownership of their own railways has not been an unqualified success and foreign ownership sometimes brought more investment. Despite this, the idea of a foreign firm owning and managing either one of the country's utilities or one of its transport networks is not a good one.

In reality if the owners and managers of a utility or a transport network are foreigners they are likely, when times are difficult, to give preference to the part of their business in their own countries rather than to the British part of it. In addition, if the utility or transport network makes a profit, it makes a difference for tax reasons whether the profit goes to our own nationals or to foreigners.

Foreign ownership and intellectual capital

In 2007, while investment in research and development increased among British-owned firms, it declined among foreign-owned firms. Another matter of concern is that foreign corporations now control 39% of British patents. In the rest of the EU non-native corporations control 13.7% of homegrown patents. In the United States the figure is 11.8% and in Japan it is 3.7%.

Another matter of concern is the transfer of a brand name owned by a British company to a foreign based company in the event of a takeover.

Affect on science and engineering in Britain

The science departments in British universities have suffered in recent years. That is an indication of the low value which Britain places on innovation and of the lack of opportunity for British graduates in the domestic market. Between 1994 and 2010, according to data from the Higher Education Policy Institution, the number of universities offering chemistry courses dropped from 83 to 66, those offering Physics courses declined from 69 to 47 and those offering material sciences degrees fell from 10 to 6. In the same period the number of universities offering media studies degrees climbed from 37 to 111. The CBI found that between 2001 and 2006 the number of electrical engineering students declined by 45%. In contrast in the period 1987 to 1997 Germany produced three to four times as many engineers as Britain. In 2008 the CBI director general noted that three quarters of Britain's engineering companies expected a shortfall in recruitment. More companies are having to recruit internationally to fill the gaps.

Britain had the first industrial revolution. Her scientists and engineers have been among the finest and most influential in the world. She owes an enormous debt of gratitude to them and to the entrepreneurs and skilled workmen that the industrial revolution brought to the fore. However, far too many of those in politics and public affairs do not feel at home in the world of industry. The one thing which these people do respect is money. The fact that Britain has experienced long years of relative peace and comparative prosperity has made them complacent. They think in the short term and short term gains are what matters to them.

Technical subjects are prone to attacks on many fronts. University courses in technical subjects are more costly to run than courses in the humanities. Therefore, the number of institutions running such courses gets less. If the number of manufacturing firms in British hands diminishes, which it has, then the opportunities for British scientists and engineers to obtain jobs in this country diminishes too. Most people, though willing to work abroad for a number of years, want to spend the predominant part of their working life in Britain. If it means that they are forced to work abroad, a career in science or engineering may become less attractive. Furthermore, the low prestige of science and engineering as careers, together with the lesser remuneration compared with that of the many other professions will deter some from choosing to follow them.

The people who have been managers of British firms throughout the years and most of the skilled personnel who work for them are not generally the most talkative of people. They are not for ever trying to get the attention of the media. Few of them would care for the razzamatazz of celebrity. That means that the successes and failures of their firms, the handicaps they have faced and the struggles they have made are not heard outside their small communities. The fact that such and such a firm was a pioneer in inventing a certain process or creating a certain product is ignored except by those who have a special interest in it. If a firm goes to the wall, its lamentations do not reach the ears of the nation at large.

What we have been witnessing is a definite bias against a significant part of the population. Certain people will want to be scientists, engineers and skilled workmen of all kinds, because these occupations are where their skills and aptitudes lie. Not everybody is suited to these occupations but a significant number of people are. To deny them the opportunity to do this or to artificially make it difficult for them is to waste a precious national resource. Let us assert strongly that their skills and aptitudes are every bit as worthwhile as those of others. They are in reality more useful to Britain than those of a lot of people.

There was a Victorian play called "Hobson's Choice". The eldest daughter of the proprietor of a shoe establishment chooses to marry the cobbler in the back room of her father's shop, rather than the fashionable sons of solicitors that her sisters chose. She prefers the cobbler because he does something real and in the process earns money. We too need to make the same choice as Miss Hobson, but it will require quite a change of sentiment to bring this about.

Manufacturing in the Far East

In this section I am heavily indebted to the book "*Made In Britain*" by Evan Davis.

The global situation in economics affects Britain, because it is not self sufficient and therefore needs to export enough goods and services to other countries to pay for its imports from them. The difference between the situation now and in the past is that previously undeveloped countries with huge populations are now busy industrialising.

Up until the last twenty or thirty years Britain was faced with competitors, such as the Germans and later the Japanese, who produced the same kinds of products as us and were often more successful at it than we were. It was never a feasible proposition for us to design products and get them manufactured in Germany or Japan. With the advent of China on the world economic scene, that has changed. China has a vast population, the majority of whom worked on the land as labourers. If these people are employed in factory jobs they will be economically better off, though of course they will earn considerably less than our own factory workers. The economics of the situation are that, if we add up the labour costs, transport costs and other incidental costs of manufacturing a high volume low technology product in China, the total costs are often considerably less than would be incurred in manufacturing the same product in Britain. This is the new situation we are faced with. The conclusion forced on us is that it is no longer at present economical for us to manufacture high volume low technology goods, unless such goods are necessary components of larger high technology products. We cannot pay our way by so doing.

However, although we may have the high volume low technology products manufactured in China, we should keep the design, research and development and marketing behind the products in Britain. This is what Dyson's have done and also Berwin & Berwin, who have chosen to have their suits manufactured in China, to the advantage of these companies and also to the advantage of Britain. The downside is the number of British workers who lost their jobs in the process.

Dyson, the inventor of the bagless vacuum cleaner, is a firm believer in the value of research. Dyson's have nearly doubled their staff in research and development in Malmesbury. They are the second biggest filer of patents in Britain after Rolls-Royce. They plough 15% of their turnover into R&D which is proportionally more than the big drug companies. Even when Dyson moved manufacturing to the Far East, research and development remained firmly based in Britain. They now employ more people in Britain than when they were manufacturing here, some 2,000, of whom 700 are engineers. Their turnover is greater and they pay more taxes. However, many of Dyson's engineers come from overseas since he finds it hard to recruit home-grown talent. In addition the company is privately owned. It is not a public limited company cited on the stock exchange and therefore not as vulnerable to a takeover.

There are a number of very successful British firms operating in this country today. Such are BAE Systems (military aircraft and other things), McLaren (racing cars), Brompton (expensive folding bicycles), GKN (engineering) and GlaxoSmith (pharmaceutical). These have taken the low volume high technology path and make few products of great value. These companies are highly automated and employ comparatively small numbers of highly motivated staff.

This situation should have led to a dramatic increase in courses in the sciences, engineering, medicine and design in Britain. Unfortunately this has not taken place. With the sale of many of our industries to foreigners, the research and development facilities previously located in Britain have often been transferred abroad. So the high technology work which would be desirable for Britain to engage in is not being done here to anything like the extent that it should be.

There will never, even in an ideal world, be enough high technology jobs to replace all the manufacturing jobs which have gone. The path of high technology is always associated with the same work being done with fewer operatives. Many of the workers displaced from manufacturing are now in service industries and this can be to the benefit of all.

However, it is not always the case that it is advisable to close down manufacturing plants in order to buy more cheaply from abroad. Those manufacturers that are still going strong have to import key components from overseas because so much of the supply chain has been fractured. One of the reasons why

Derby based Bombardier lost out to Siemens on the Thameslink train system contract was the dearth of local suppliers of vital component parts. The manufacture of things is not an isolated activity. A firm, which is supplying a product to its customers, itself needs to buy its constituent components from a number of other firms. There is a state of mutual dependence here. If any one part of the association of firms doing business with each other is not present, then something has to be ordered from outside the country. The advantage of being able to obtain everything you need locally is lost. The damage of manufacturing or expertise being transferred out of Britain affects not only the particular company to which this happens but also all those firms associated with it.

Perhaps a good proportion of all the decline in British manufacturing is not inevitable at all, but is due to a fanatical opposition to giving proper protection and help to British firms. A watching brief needs to be taken on cases of firms deciding to do their manufacturing abroad. Is it totally justifiable on economic grounds or are strategic issues warranting thinking twice about it? In some cases it could be justifiable to finance the re-establishment of a network of small firms.

The market ideology

Some people think that the market can do no wrong. If the action of market forces produces a certain result, it cannot be questioned. There is the assumption of a level playing field. However, there are circumstances when not even the existence of a level playing field would persuade me to accept the action of market forces. It also assumes that the market rewards merit and ensures the survival of the fittest. Such a view is naive. The reality is very different.

When a company goes public, it obtains cash by floating shares in it on the stock exchange, which are then bought up by individuals who have faith in the company. When the company is doing well the value of the shares increases and when it is doing badly the value of the shares goes down. When the company is doing well more people are likely to buy its shares and when it is doing badly fewer people are likely to do this. Furthermore, when the company is doing badly people are more likely to sell their shares in it, unless they remain convinced of the long term value of the company. This is a simple analysis of the system. It is complicated by the fact that many of the investors in a public company are institutional investors rather than individuals. It is also complicated by the advent of some dubious practices which I will discuss later.

In the old days, before Big Bang in the Thatcherite era, there were not many takeovers of British companies by foreigners. The vast majority of British public companies were British owned. Further if one British company was taken over by another, or if there was an amalgamation of smaller companies to form a larger one, there was usually a good commercial reason for it. In the case of a takeover it could be that the company taken over was in trouble. In the case of an amalgamation the larger company which emerged was thought to be more competitive. Asset stripping, while not unknown, was not prevalent. While not perfect, this could be said to be a good system.

The advent of Big Bang did away with many of the old restrictions and gave rise to a much more aggressive form of capitalism. Also, since London became less restrictive than New York, much American business moved to London, which attracted the Continental Europeans as well. Further most of the old City firms of merchant bankers were taken over by foreigners.

There has now come into being the practice of using debt to finance takeover bids. We are told that this is all part of globalisation and that the abolition of restrictions has made the City of London a global powerhouse, which earns the British treasury a lot of money in tax. A gambling casino is a very profitable enterprise, but the proliferation of them throughout the country is strictly controlled.

Individuals and institutions who make it their business to live off unsecured debt, even though it is wrapped up in very sophisticated ways, are living on shifting sand. There is a time when the debt may be called in and the debtor may not have the money to pay it. A system based on unsecured debt does not last for ever, a fact that recent years have clearly underlined.

Meanwhile, perfectly good British companies have been made the sacrificial lambs for this sort of behaviour. The whole business of trying to make money out of sophisticated manipulation of unsecured debt is by its very nature unsustainable. By contrast the British firms who were sacrificed represented hard work, solid worth and steady sustainable prospects. To sell such firms was easy, but to recover them or to recreate them is considerably more difficult.

Important aspects of takeovers

Almost all the takeovers of British companies by foreign ones, which have been described earlier in this chapter have been financed by debt. The British companies concerned were in good shape. ICI, Pilkington's, the software company Autonomy, P&O, Thames Water, Arriva, Cadbury, Boots and many others were all prospering. Indeed their attractiveness for their new owners was that they were worth acquiring. The takeovers could not have taken place if the predator companies had not borrowed large sums of money. A lot of people will find this to be totally unacceptable. The workers of these companies were often the losers. The boards of the firms taken over gained financially and so did the shareholders.

Another aspect of the takeovers of British firms by foreigners is that in a great many cases the predator company was a competitor. The motivation for the takeover was in many cases just to remove the competition. In such cases the freedom of investors to profit from the situation must surely take second place to saving the victim from such an eventuality.

Assets to be preserved

A British company domiciled in this country pays full corporation tax to the treasury. If a company is registered elsewhere, even if its operations are here, this will not be the case. Really it would be desirable if any company operating in this country paid full corporation tax, which would happen if the company was operating in Switzerland. The same thing should apply in Britain.

If a British company passes into foreign ownership, the control on what it will do or will not do passes also. At the very least it would be desirable if any research and development carried out by the company in Britain should remain here, but at present there is no guarantee of this. Further the personnel here may lose their jobs. Many of these could be skilled jobs. The part of the company still in Britain could become merely an assembly or distribution company. At present none of these damaging possibilities are prevented by law. Sometimes the new foreign owner may make a promise, which can be reneged upon in a year or two. Unless an eventuality is forbidden by law, it may very easily happen. But even if something is forbidden by law, a new foreign owner may consider it worthwhile to disobey the law and pay the fine.

The passing of one or more British companies into foreign ownership may mean that Britain loses its expertise in a particular industrial field. On the other hand when a British company takes over an American company, as sometimes happens, the American company will be only one of many in that particular industry and there will be no great loss of

American expertise in that particular field. The difference in the two situations needs to be recognised.

There are also strategic considerations. Common sense would dictate not allowing any company involved in defence being taken over by a foreign concern. Also what is necessary for Britain's survival as an independent country should be in British hands. The infrastructure of a country and that includes all the utilities should be maintained by the country of origin. The fact that our water, gas and electricity are in foreign hands is very unfortunate. Our ports, railways and airports should be in British hands. The whole purpose of the foreign concern buying the utility is to make money. The satisfaction of the new customers is a secondary consideration. Where there is a conflict between satisfying their new customers and their own compatriots, it is not surprising if the latter come first.

Before a takeover is contemplated, any British company ought to be in a better position for a significant amount of time after the takeover than it was previously. There should be as much or more research and development, employment of personnel, skilled or otherwise and the sales figures should be higher. Also, Britain should not lose tax revenue from the takeover. These are guidelines, but it is essential that the persons judging these matters should be thoroughly knowledgeable about the business.

Manufacturing makes sense

For those people who say that manufacturing decline is inevitable, Professor Bush in his publication "*Produce And Prosper*" cites the examples of Germany and the Republic of Ireland.

"In 2005 Germany (population 83 million) overtook the USA (population 300 million) as the world's largest trading nation. This has entirely come about by continued expansion in the export of manufactured goods. Within that surge, Germany is now far and away the largest exporter of machinery, being responsible for around 25% of the world's supply (in China, India, Europe and the Americas). Germany has achieved this surge by (a) support of German manufacturing industry in all its trade negotiations, (b) a comprehensive system of education and training, particularly at technician level, (c) an industry- supporting culture in the financial and economics media."

"In just under 30 years the Republic of Ireland has increased its industrial output per capita (mainly manufacturing) from two thirds of the 1979 UK figure to 70% more than the 2005 UK figure. At the same time Ireland's GDP per capita has increased from about 50% of the UK's in 1979 to approximately 20% greater than the UK's in 2005, while its exports of goods has risen to about 30% of Britain's with a population of about 6.5% of Britain's. While Ireland is currently experiencing the effects of overblown credit expansion as in Britain, the basic facts of its achievement relative to Britain are unaffected."

However, the above statements are not quite as overwhelming as they seem. Part of the success of the Republic of Ireland has been due to the injection of money from the EU. While part of the comparative success of Germany, as compared with the United States is due to the fact that Germany has a greater need to export than the latter, which has a much larger internal market. Nevertheless in spite of these advantages, the facts cited above about Germany and the Republic of Ireland need to be noted.

The protectionism of foreign countries

Countries such as France, Germany, Spain and the United States all have different forms of "economic patriotism" in place, which make foreign takeovers of local companies difficult to achieve.

In France widespread state holdings in vital utilities act as a brake on deals. The French think it is in the national interest to prevent key technologies falling into foreign hands. There is a published list of industries, including defence, which France shields from foreign takeovers. When the American drinks giant PepsiCola was trying in 2005 to bid for the food firm Danone, President Chirac declared that it was to be considered as a "strategic" company and so safe from takeover. Spain has worked hard to ensure that the country's energy companies remain Spanish. It thwarted the bid in 2006 by the German energy group E.ON for Endesa. The Swiss too have kept Nestle safe from foreign prowlers.

Germany, where private equity companies leading the takeover revolution have been described as "locusts", is similarly resistant to foreign involvement. It has a vast collection of medium-sized businesses that have remained in family control for generations. These are focused on long-term survival rather than short-term profit. The family element means that firms are largely immune to tinkering of the kind undertaken in Britain and are more focused on investment. Vodafone's takeover of Mannesmann in April 2000 is one of the few hostile deals ever to have been completed in Germany. That country's caution even extends to enterprises seeking to just establish a foothold. There was concern when Dubai International Financial Centre bought a 2.2% stake in Deutsche Bank in 2007 and in 2010 when the Russians sought to win a stake in Deutsche Telecom. The German response to this was to pass a law that allows the government to veto foreign investment of 25% or more in a company if such a venture is deemed to be a national security threat.

The United States, which likes to present itself as a "champion" of free trade does not adopt a *laissez-faire* approach in its own backyard. Foreigners are not allowed to buy American airlines. Overseas shareholders are only allowed to own 25%. Television networks are also protected. That is one reason why Rupert Murdoch took on American citizenship. Oil is also protected. China's state-owned oil company was prevented from purchasing the struggling oil firm Unocal in 2005. In Canada too, when in 2010 the London-quoted mining giant BHP Billiton launched a bid for the Saskatchewan-based fertiliser group Potash Corporation, the state of Saskatchewan put enormous pressure on the Canadian government, so that the bid was ruled out. Moreover, while India has bought UK companies like Jaguar Rover, it has not allowed British firms to take majority control in the country's financial sector. Japan places the national interest above that of the individual or the investor. It has therefore proved to be very difficult to penetrate by foreign companies.

Prospects for British industry

There is one advantage of the present industrial scene over that of the sixties and seventies. Today firms employ smaller numbers and employees are highly skilled. There is not the same danger of strikes and demarcation disputes that there was at that time.

In order to prevent absolutely the foreign takeover, as distinct from investment in British companies designated as strategic businesses, the government could take a controlling proportion of the shares. For instance the Norwegian Government has taken a 30% interest in their principal oil rig engineering company, Aker Kvaerner, specifically to prevent Russia's Gazprom from acquiring it. Russia itself has a commission which has the complete right to block a foreign firm from taking shares in a Russian company. France and Germany employ informal means to obstruct foreign takeovers. The USA is considering new legislation in the field.

In considering whether a particular company is of strategic value to Britain, it should also be asked whether it is the sole representative of a certain field of industry in this country. If so, its value should be considered to be strategic.

Once Britain was free from the EU, the government could legislate to limit the proportion of shares which a foreign concern could obtain in particular classes of British companies. It could also legislate to prevent any utility company falling into foreign hands. It could be beneficial in the long term for the government (if there was any spare cash available) or appropriate British companies to buy back utilities from their foreign owners.

Where there is any thought of resurrecting industries which have gone to the wall, any previous employee with knowledge and experience to contribute should be invited to do so with financial remuneration for his or her time. Every effort should be made to return companies taken over by foreign concerns, particularly where they are strategically important, to British ownership. If the treasury needs to spend money in this task, then so be it.

In cases where there is no great objection to a takeover of a British company on strategic grounds, there could be legislation forbidding the reduction of the workforce by a certain amount in the first five years after the takeover. Similarly there could be a requirement that a significant amount of the research and development of the company taken over should remain in Britain.

There should be a definite separation between retail (high street banks) and investment banks, that retail banks should only be allowed to take deposits from private and commercial customers and advance loans to that same group up to the limit of their deposits. Investment banks will be free to raise money by bonds and shares, but will not be allowed to be deposit-takers. This separation is already starting.

The functions of retail banks and building societies should be separate as in the past. This would enable the high street banks to do the job which they once did of giving service to customers and loans to small businesses, leaving building societies to deal with mortgages. A really close connection between firms and high street banks like there is in Germany is also desirable.

Public authorities of all kinds including government departments should be legally obliged to buy British unless there is an overwhelming reason not to. This would stop the House of Commons ordering china from a German company rather than from the perfectly good British contenders.

Universities and colleges should be prohibited from closing down departments of science or engineering and those already closed down should be re-opened. Public funds should be made available to enable this to take place.

British students should be given financial incentives to study technical subjects, such as physics, chemistry, material science, engineering, the biological sciences, medicine and computer science. Lower level study of technical subjects should be given similar incentives. There should be a significant increase in industrial apprenticeships, financed if necessary by the government. Liaison between universities and industry should be encouraged. Firms should be given financial incentives to give in house training to British students where necessary.

The discipline in state schools together with their academic quality needs to be improved and the fashionable trendy approach rejected. We could find in the education system of Germany much to emulate.

There needs to be a close relationship between firms and banks, as exists in Germany.

The government needs to choose the exchange rate of the currency and interest rates and taxes in general such as to give maximum help to enable British industry to flourish and to export.

There needs to be an end to the short term outlook and the

lure of the quick profit. If measures such as the above are taken, British industry could rise from the ashes and have a bright future.

3

Immigration and Allied Topics

Overseas aid

The present government has up till now protected expenditure on overseas aid from the cuts which it is imposing in other areas, although there are indications that the policy may be altered. Previous governments have been equally enthusiastic about it. It is assumed that overseas aid benefits the ordinary people in other lands whom it is supposed to benefit. The amount this country gives in overseas aid is presented as an indication of how generous and enlightened the government is, and it gives the organisers of the various aid programmes pleasant jobs and life styles.

In many cases the giving of overseas aid is absurd. British aid to India has been attacked by the finance minister of that country. He said it was demeaning and futile. India today is wealthy enough to have a space programme and nuclear weapons. It has more millionaires than Britain. Aid is also given to Pakistan in spite of the fact that it has unofficially been helping the Taliban in Afghanistan. Despite Brazil now having its own aid programme and enjoying a far larger economy than Britain, £13 million was given to it by us in the past decade. Despite the sabre rattling of the Argentine government over the Falklands, £7 million was given to that country between 2007 and 2013 as part of an EU support package and £20 million since 2000 via the International Monetary Fund. Between 2000 and 2010 Britain gave £3.3 million to Ecuador, in spite of the hostility shown to Britain about a recent diplomatic matter. In 2010/2011 £97 million of British aid was spent in Latin America up from £84 million in 2007/2008.

There are a lot of poor countries in Africa.They are real countries with real people. They have been independent of colonial rule for some time, some of them for as much as fifty years. Since independence their true characters have become evident. In some cases tribalism has come to the fore. Some of these countries have become dictatorships with the wealth of the country going to the governing elite. Some have experienced civil war. That was the fate of Angola, the Sudan, Ethiopia, the Congo, Nigeria at the time of the Biafran breakaway and others. There has even been genocide in the conflicts of Rwanda and Burundi. For a time Zimbabwe, formerly Rhodesia,and South Africa were under white rule. Whatever else was wrong with it, poverty was not a characteristic of that period. Most Western aid given to these countries has tended to go to the ruling elite. In Ethiopia during the famine at the time of the civil war most of the aid went to the Ethiopian army. Often the form of aid given has been inappropriate. Sometimes the giving of Western aid has been to the detriment of local producers making it uneconomic for them to stay in business. It has even been reported that children and others have been mutilated so as to make them objects of pity to extract aid from Westerners.

A case of £21 million of aid given to Rwanda hit the news recently. The aid was used by the local dictator to oppress his own people. Some of our politicians had visited that country and had hobnobbed with him. The exercise was meant to display their caring credentials.

What, if any, of the aid sponsored by the British government actually helps those whom it is supposed to help, and what is just flattering the egos of the politicians or providing employment to those in charge of projects?

Aid given by Western voluntary organisations is in a different category and often does real good. There is the work of Medecins Sans Frontières. The medical treatment of people with disabilities from Third World countries in order to give them a new quality of life is definitely worthwhile. Aid to provide fresh water to impoverished areas is of genuine benefit. The aid given by voluntary organisations is directed to specific targets and everybody concerned knows exactly what the aid is financing. Furthermore, this has nothing to do with the government sponsored overseas aid, which could well be abolished.

Much of the motivation behind overseas aid comes from comparing the lot of the people in these underdeveloped countries with ourselves. The assumption is that we are developed, rich and happy and they are undeveloped, poor and unhappy. This is too simplistic and often lacking in respect for those people. Unless we can offer them very specific benefits, it would be better to leave them alone.

Overseas wars

There is a paradox in the attitudes of the liberal establishment. People who are vociferous in being against the mildest form of racialism in Britain are quite happy to support bombing the hell out of the inhabitants of underdeveloped countries, because their governments do not conform to our ideals of democracy.

These so-called liberals are very keen on telling foreigners in their own countries what to do, but if these same foreigners migrate to Britain they utterly refrain from telling them what to do here, because here we have embraced multiculturalism.

This makes no sense at all. Britain is the country where we have control. We have no control in foreign countries and precious little influence either.

Things may have been different in the days of the British Empire, when we actually had personnel in these countries who knew something about them and who were in fact governing them. Even then there were limits to what we could do. Today things are different. We do not have the knowledge of or any lasting commitment to any country other than our own. In fact where the West has intervened militarily in underdeveloped countries recently the results have often made a bad situation worse.

There is a lot of naivety behind this urge to intervene militarily in foreign countries. The so-called liberals assume that everything is rosy in the world except in the particular place where they have chosen to intervene. In reality there are plenty of countries in the world today whose governments we would regard as barbaric or questionable. This is not likely to change because we want it to. Sometimes we assist the rebels against a despotic regime in for example the Middle East. When the rebels in their turn become despotic and unsavoury, Western liberals are very surprised. They should not have been so naive in the first place.

Tony Blair during his period in office was responsible for three foreign interventions: in Serbia on behalf of the Kosovans, in Iraq and in Afghanistan. The Western military intervention in the latter was unwinnable and anyone who knew their history would say so. In Iraq we exchanged the rule of one dictator for unceasing bloodshed and inter- religious strife. To prefer the Kosovans to the Serbians shows ignorance and naivety. Furthermore, these military interventions were costly in both men and money. For Blair these adventures enabled him to pose as a statesman on the world stage. A cynic might comment that he did quite well financially from it also.

This Western readiness to intervene militarily in foreign countries dates back to just after the fall of Soviet communism. During the Cold War the West tended to limit its interventions to what was necessary to contain communism and promote Western interests in the global conflict. After the end of the Cold War the West felt less constrained and able to do something more. It hit on the idea of promoting democracy throughout the world, but if any non-Western country is going to become democratic and politically benign in the Western sense it must want to do so. If it does not want to do so, then no amount of Western intervention will persuade it otherwise.

Sometimes it is necessary to intervene militarily in foreign countries to protect British interests. Such intervention must be necessary to secure definite objectives and those objectives must be obtainable. Otherwise, they are a waste of the lives of military personnel and of considerable sums of money, which could be better spent on other things.

Health tourism

A particular case illustrates this problem. An emergency caesarean was carried out recently at Wythenshawe Hospital in Manchester. The mother had her baby and when she had recovered, left. The cost is thought to have been around £10,000. But the woman does not live in Britain and is a Nigerian citizen. She travelled from her home in Lagos to Manchester Airport, jumped in a taxi when she landed and turned up at A&E. She said that an ultrasound scan had revealed complications and she wanted to be in "safe hands". The hospital said that she needed midwives, two urology consultants, a radiologist, two anaesthetists and two obstetric consultants in the course of her treatment. She was presented with a bill, but she left no address, so there is no means of tracing her. This is not an isolated case but a major problem in the NHS. Estimates as to how much it costs us vary. In *The Daily Mail* (4th April 2013), Professor Thomas, a consultant surgeon at the Royal Marsden Hospital in London said that he thought the cost to the NHS could run into billions. There has been one successful prosecution of an Egyptian called Albert Girgis, who had cost more than £30,000 in heart surgery and drugs.

This health tourism puts extra strain on the NHS. According to John Reid, Health Minister in the last government, "Every time that happens somebody has to wait a little longer, often in pain, to get the service to which they are entitled". Foreigners, including failed asylum seekers, were effectively stealing treatment from the people of Britain. As John Reid continued, "If there are bona fide tourists ill in the street, of course we will do what we have to do but we are not mugs. There is a difference between being civilised and being taken for a ride".

What can be done about it? There is no centralised system through which hospitals can check patients' eligibility. However, West Middlesex Hospital, close to Heathrow Airport, demand that foreign patients pay before any treatment is given. Unfortunately no other hospital seems to have done the same.

There was a proposal that immigrants from developing countries should be tested for HIV before receiving visas (there was evidence that some were coming here solely to receive the best treatment), but this was dropped because of allegations of racism. In fact the proposal makes good sense.

Health tourism should be stopped in spite of the opposition to this on humanitarian grounds. People from abroad should be charged before being given medical treatment. Britain cannot be doctor and nursemaid to the entire world. It has not got the resources to do this. Further the first duty of Britain is to its own citizens. The care of the citizens of other countries is the responsibility of their own governments.

Asylum seekers

Asylum seekers may deserve to be admitted on humanitarian grounds. In the past the Huguenots, fleeing persecution in France, and the Jews fleeing pogroms in Russia and later fleeing Nazi persecution, were rightly admitted on these grounds. Later in the Seventies the Uganda Asians were admitted, although in their case an alternative venue could have been the Indian subcontinent. Dissidents from Communist countries fleeing to the West during the Cold War were another example of genuine asylum seekers.

Most people of normal human sympathies would have no quarrel with the admission of any of the above. The persecution from which they were fleeing was undoubtedly genuine. Unfortunately the need for asylum for people fleeing persecution has not abated. In all cases it is necessary to check that there is a genuine case for asylum. Even when the case is genuine, the rule is now that the request for asylum should be made to the first country through which the asylum seeker passes in his or her escape.

In fact the proportion of genuine asylum seekers among the immigrants to Britain is comparatively small. The vast majority of the immigrants to this country in the last twenty years or more have not been asylum seekers but economic migrants, attracted to Britain for economic reasons and by the generous benefits available from the welfare system. These people cannot be criticised for this. In their place we would have done the same. It is our own authorities who have admitted them who are to blame. We cannot afford to be a benefactor to the entire world. No country can afford to do this.

As well as bogus asylum seekers, there are people subject to deportation from Britain who claim that they would be mistreated if they were sent back to their countries of origin. If you are going to take advantage of the liberal institutions of this country, then firstly you should not have broken the law either here or abroad and secondly you are logically obliged to be in favour of our liberal institutions. In very many cases individuals who despise and detest them seek to take advantage of them when resisting deportation. This should no longer be allowed.

Racialism

Does the concept of racialism have any practical use? If a person from one ethnic group murders a person from another ethnic group, that is murder, which we condemn. It is not relevant that the killer and the killed were from different ethnic groups. Supposing a person from one ethnic group accuses a person of another ethnic group of something which is not true. Then that is false testimony of one person against another, which again we condemn. It is not relevant that the two parties were from different ethnic groups. Either the behaviour of one person to another is okay, or it is not okay. The concept of racialism is unnecessary.

In spite of what I have said above, people of one ethnic group may be prejudiced against those of another. The prejudice may be justified or not. If the prejudice exists because of past wrongs, then it can be said to be justified, but if the prejudice is simply because of characteristics which those of the other ethnic group cannot help having, then it is not justified. In so far as racialism is a valid concept, it must refer to the latter.

When one person has a legitimate cause for quarrel with another, that quarrel should not be made illegitimate merely because the individuals are from different ethnic groups. Today accusations of racialism are often made over relatively trivial matters. Friction between two or more people in society can occur, whether the participants are from the same ethnic groups or from different ethnic groups. Provided the friction does not involve violence, it should not be a cause for great concern.

From time to time nowadays the fact that someone is of a different ethnic group to the majority is made an excuse when they are accused of crime or unacceptable behaviour. This attitude is wrong. We must have one law for everybody in this country.

Immigrants as cheap labour

Some people say that the immigrants take jobs which the locals no longer want to do. A moment's thought will reveal that this is grossly misleading.

Before the coming of the immigrants in large numbers all these so-called unpopular jobs were done by locals. But when done by locals the employers had to pay a satisfactory wage. When done by immigrants the employers could get away with paying significantly less. That explains the attraction of immigrants in the eyes of a lot of people.

Our own people

Let us draw attention to the vast majority of the British people.

They have fought in our wars, they have worked in our factories and down in our mines and toiled in our fields. They have been people who do not leave their mark. They have been in our country for generations and they regard newcomers as newcomers. In the unprecedented mass immigration of the last fifteen years - an immigration to which they never gave their consent - there have been a lot of newcomers.

It is our own ordinary people who have faced competition for jobs from newcomers who will work for less. It is they who face competition for housing from the newcomers. Often they will be competing for the remaining council houses. It is the newcomers who often buy up houses to let to as many tenants as they can possibly fit in, thus changing the character of neighbourhoods. The vast influx of newcomers has inevitably greatly increased the pressure on the NHS, making the service less good for our own people. Education has also suffered forcing our own people to be educated together with people whose English is a second language. The idea that the UK should have to provide translations of official documents for the benefit of immigrants, rather than making it their responsibility to understand these documents is misconceived. Added to this is the cost to the UK taxpayers'. Law and order has deteriorated, since the police, even when they are not subject to time wasting form filling, do not know their neighbourhoods like they used to in the past. Among the newcomers have been foreign gangs who should have been deported but are not, thus making the situation worse. It is also ordinary people who are often made redundant when their firms suffer a takeover

The so-called liberals do not seem to realise that Britain is a small country, which already had as great a population as it could cope with. Obviously mass immigration would be a bad idea. If the newcomers have contributed to the economy, that is more than made up for by the extra pressure on our social services. It also inevitably makes the country more crowded.

The better off are shielded from the effects of mass immigration on ordinary people. Better off people can live in pleasant and expensive neighbourhoods, where crime is not a great problem. They can send their children to private schools or to select schools in the state system. They can go private for their health. On top of everything the better off are more adept at using the system to their advantage than their poorer cousins. Therefore, these better off people can sing the praises of mass immigration as being ever so liberal and ever so politically correct.

There were and are a whole number of problems in our society:

Housing and jobs, particularly for young people.

The condition of the state education system.

The state of the NHS.

The amount of crime in our society.

Every one of these problem areas has been made more difficult to cope with by the recent mass immigration into this country. Most adversely affected by it are the poorest and most vulnerable sections of our society.

A country is not a hotel

There are a great number of different peoples in the world. Sometimes these peoples are described as tribes, sometimes they are organised politically in nation states and sometimes the link between groups is their adherence to a certain religion. Particular peoples are mostly associated with particular geographical areas. You would generally expect to find Indians in India and British people in Britain. The immigration of Indians to Britain is a recent phenomenon. Though Muslims have in recent years immigrated to European countries, Islam is most associated with the Middle East and parts of Asia, just as Christianity is associated with Britain, the rest of Europe, the Americas and Australasia. It is true that the Americas and Australasia are in fact almost entirely made up of immigrants, but that is a fact peculiar to them and not the rule in other parts of the world. However, the United States, Canada, Australia and New Zealand have been and still are very particular as to whom they admit as immigrants and are very keen on instilling into them allegiance to their adopted country.

The natural thing is for the peoples of the world to inhabit different geographical areas. It is because they have been separated from one another by geography that they have evolved different cultures. The evolution of these cultures has been strongly influenced by the politics of the regions where they flourish. Some of these cultures have remained relatively static over long periods of time up to the present day. Others have developed dramatically over the centuries and could be said to be still developing today.

A country like Britain has developed dramatically over the centuries. The majority of its people will describe themselves as being some form of Christian, but Christianity is just one of the influences contributing to the national character. And though Christianity is important and should be respected, there are other parts of the character of Britain and its people which are even more important for determining who is genuinely British.

There is democracy and the various struggles that parts of its population have waged to achieve recognition as equals. The concept of an over-riding theocracy is not accepted here. There is the position of women, which was always higher than that in many parts of the world and which has forged right ahead in the last century. The advanced position of women in Britain is not just a minor characteristic, but central to the very fabric of our society. Furthermore, the supreme value accorded to the individual, if not always adhered to in practice, is universally recognised by the British as a desirable ideal. This means that, though a potential immigrant to Britain may practise a different religion to Christianity, it is essential that he or she should feel bound by these other attributes of being British.

Now there are very many immigrants who fully accept our way of life and our mores of behaviour. They can be said to be fully westernised. They speak English fluently and make use of the cultural advantages of being in Britain. Some of them join our armed forces and to them we owe a special debt of gratitude. Some of them have competed for Britain in the Olympics. Others of them have taken part in our television programmes. None of these people can be said to be just here for the state benefits.

A country is not the same as a hotel. Anybody can come to a hotel without any profession of allegiance to the country where it is situated and without any evidence of compatibility with its citizens. A country is different. The native citizens of that country may have an opinion as to whether you will be welcome as a fellow citizen or not. It should not be forgotten that the introduction of Europeans in large numbers to places like Kenya and Algeria in colonial times was much resented by the African inhabitants. We should not expect our own people to feel differently. If you are going to become a citizen of a country, not your own, for best results you need to fit in. Using elementary common sense, it is not difficult for the average fair minded person to determine whether particular immigrants fit into the category of those who accept our mores and way of life and speak English reasonably well, or whether they do not. It is fair minded common sense which is needed here, not political correctness. Using the former, it would not be difficult to determine who should be welcomed to remain in this country and who should not.

A challenge to multiculturalism

Today the doctrine of multiculturalism is espoused by many people claiming to be ultra liberal. It favours a multiplicity of cultures in Britain, regardless of whether any of them are compatible with British norms evolved throughout its history.

Whereas many immigrants from overseas are perfectly at home with the norms of British society and indeed welcome them, there are others whose practices and attitudes are very different, such as the following:

Honour killings when a girl behaves in too Westernised a fashion.

The forcing of their daughters to marry men whom they, the parents, have chosen.

The subjection of girls to undergo the barbaric practice of female circumcision.

The advocacy of or practise of polygamy.

The clothing of wives and daughters in the burka, thus entirely hiding their faces. The latter practice is sometimes defended as being an expression of the wearer's religion, but it is perfectly clear that it is really a sign of male subjugation of females. When people in the West wear particular clothing as an expression of their religion, it never covers their faces.

Some of them prey upon Western girls as being easier to subject to their desires than girls from their own culture.

The perpetrating of terrorist acts against Jewish interests as an expression of hostility to the actions of the Israeli government.

The going to foreign countries with the intention of training to be a terrorist, or enlisting in extremist organisations either in Britain or abroad.

It is perfectly clear that the practices described above are diametrically opposed to the norms of British society in addition to often being against the law. Moreover, the establishment of these norms is the result of successful struggles throughout British history. Can we exempt some of our citizens from compliance with these norms. The answer must be no. People who engage in the practices described above or approve of them can by no stretch of the imagination be considered as really British. They could however be an accepted part of the societies from which they originally came. If they remain here, efforts to change their practices and attitudes would in reality be futile. The solution is that they should return to their countries of origin. That would be the best outcome for all parties.

The attitude of the authorities is often a desire not to become involved. They are afraid of offending the so-called leaders of some of these ethnic communities if they assert Western values. They are inclined to turn a blind eye to the sufferings of the female victims of misogynist behaviour. An example of a prominent member of the establishment taking this kind of attitude was displayed by the last Archbishop of Canterbury willing to condone the practice of Sharia law in this country. He was trying to be liberal, but he was ignoring the implications of what he proposed.

The attitude of Western liberals is contradictory. Two of the most fundamental tenets of the West are the equal rights of men and women and the rights of the individual as distinct from family or tribe. Western liberals who do not understand that multiculturalism is not compatible with adherence to the above principles, are deceiving themselves.

In the past our leaders were much more willing to assert

British values. We recall the campaigns to abolish Suttee and female infanticide in India at the time of the British Raj. We also recall the long battle of the British against the Arab Slave Trade in Africa, not to mention our previous campaigns against our own slave trade and against slavery as such in the British Empire. None of these endeavours were deterred by the fear of offending powerful people, whether they were foreigners or our own people. It is not just the British who were keen on Western values, the ruler of Turkey after the 1st World War was Kemal Ataturk. He deliberately introduced Western norms and was responsible to a large extent for emancipating Turkish women.

The situation today is that we no longer have power outside our own country and it is futile to delude ourselves that we have. We do have power in Britain if we wish to use it. In Britain we have the power to enforce our norms if we care to. I ask myself whom I admire most, these stalwart and courageous Victorian forbears or their successors of today.

Militant Islam

It must be made clear from the start that the religion itself is not a problem. Provided people accept the cultural norms of this country and behave in an acceptable way, they should not be discriminated against because of their religion.

However, many people of this religion do have attitudes and practices which are incompatible with Western norms. As I have said earlier, such people should not be in this country and if it were not for certain economic benefits, they would probably have remained in their countries of origin. Moreover, while they are here, they may act in a way incompatible with Western norms and may put pressure on their more Westernised coreligionists to conform to their views.

The history of Islam has been imperialistic, quite as much as the history of Christianity. But Christianity has evolved together with the countries in which it has flourished. It has had to cope with the Renaissance, the Reformation, the Enlightenment, the French and Russian Revolutions, the Industrial Revolution and Parliamentary Democracy. Islam has only had to cope with these things at second hand, if at all. It is fair to say that Islam is still in imperialistic mode with a fanatical devotion not seen in the West since the Middle Ages.

There is a determination in our society to avoid giving offense to the Muslim community in any way, an attitude which is not extended to any other community residing in Britain. This is partly due to a wish to avoid violent retaliation from Muslims and is partly due to the existence in the world today of states in the Middle East flush with oil. Both these factors have made successive governments unjustifiably timid. Quite frankly terrorists or people who are likely to be terrorists should be deported. As for reactions from foreign Muslim states, it should be made clear to them that they rule the roost in their own lands, whereas we rule the roost in ours.

There is an interesting parallel which deserves our consideration. Let us take ourselves back to the time of the Cold War, when Russian nationals, unless they had fled to the West as dissidents, were regarded with suspicion. Can we imagine the government of the day allowing large numbers of Russian nationals to come here to live, unless they had been clearly proved to be asylum seekers. The answer is no. It is a pity that the parallel is not drawn with many of our present day immigrants.

The politics of immigration

One reason why the Blair/Brown government allowed the mass immigration which occurred during that time was because they thought that the immigrants would be long time Labour voters. They were probably right about that, but putting that aside, the mass immigration will certainly alter the political complexion of Britain. It will alter it even more if the immigrants reproduce at a greater rate than the majority community. This will be so even if immigration into the country was stopped tomorrow. So, if more immigrants continue to arrive, this alteration of the political complexion of Britain will be even greater.

Britain will change in two ways. Firstly, its total population will increase, putting a greater strain on its resources and making the country more crowded. Secondly, a substantial proportion of the population will have different values to those of the majority community. In those places in Britain which are most densely populated by the immigrants the culture is similar to or identical with that of the countries where the immigrants came from. When they enter parts of Britain today, native British people feel as if they are visiting a foreign country. So Britain will no longer be the product of the political and cultural activities of the British people over the centuries, but a polyglot place over which they have no control.

It has been and is the desire of every country in the world to govern itself and to be independent. The independence of Britain has been reduced by its membership of the EU. That independence has also been further reduced by the mass immigration which has occurred in recent years. To deny this because of notions of political correctness is to refuse to face realities. It will be a sad day when, if members of these immigrant communities start calling the shots politically, some of our people resort to violence as the only way to save Britain. If such a thing were to occur, the proper people to blame would be those naive self righteous liberals who were responsible for the unrestricted mass immigration in the first place.

Practical measures concerning immigration

The first of the practical measures for dealing with immigration is to deport all illegal immigrants. We would also have to take action against the gangs who bring people to

Britain for profit. We will need sufficient specially trained personnel to enforce these measures and this will involve the expenditure of a substantial amount of money, as will the enforcement of most other measures concerning immigration.

The second practical measure involves Britain leaving the EU. This would mean that all EU citizens in Britain would immediately become foreigners, with no right to continue to remain in the country except as aliens and with no right to claim British benefits. This would mean that we could deport large numbers of Eastern Europeans who have come here in recent years. We would also be saved from the expected influx of large numbers of Romanians and Bulgarians.

The third measure is to deport all those guilty of taking part in or aiding and abetting the practices described in the section entitled “A challenge to muliculturalism”. Further the automatic right of wives to join their husbands in Britain should be made dependent on their having a reasonable ability to speak English. If a marriage was contracted solely to enable a wife from abroad to come to Britain, she should be refused entry. This would indicate a determination to enforce British norms of conduct. To be able to do this, without running the risk of being prosecuted by the EU, Britain would need to leave that organisation.

The fourth measure would be to facilitate (with financial help if appropriate) the resettlement in their countries of origin of all those who for cultural reasons disapprove of the British way of life. The logic is that if they really disapprove of it and prefer their ancestral ways, they should go to countries where their ancestral ways are more the norm. It would be helpful if we could obtain the collaboration of the governments of their countries of origin for this purpose, and it would make sense to give financial aid to these countries on condition that they accepted these people.

The fifth measure would be to grade the entitlement to

social security benefits, council housing and use of the services of the NHS according to the length of stay in this country. Those who had been here for thirty years or more or those who had parents or grandparents of British nationality would get full benefits and entitlements. Those who had only been here between thirty years and twenty years would get lower rates of benefit, those who had been here between twenty years and ten years would get even less and those who had been here less than ten years would get nothing at all. The provisions suggested here are merely suggestions. The important idea is the graduation of entitlement to benefits with length of stay in the country. This would be an effective way of dealing with economic migrants.

4

The Green Issues

Reasonable care for the environment

A lot of people have an affection for the environment and for our natural habitat.

We care for the fate of endangered species of animals and plants. We think of the the orangutan, the giant panda and also understand that their habitats are being destroyed by the burning of the rain forests by commercial interests who want to turn them into agricultural land. Of course we need to take into consideration the food requirements of growing populations, but we hope that a happy mean can be found between the two sets of interests. Sometimes the rain forests are being destroyed to make way for the growing of biofuels. That is quite indefensible and it exposes the falsity of the claim of biofuels to be a green option. Often the reason for the destruction of the rain forest is purely the financial advantage of commercial interests, without any consideration for the ecology of the entire area and indeed of the world. This is deeply regrettable, but the responsibility for it lies with the Brazilian government, not with anyone else and certainly not with Britain.

Another example of the threat to endangered species is the killing of African elephants and rhinos for the sake of the ivory in their tusks and horns. Apparently the ivory is much prized in the Far East. Like many others, I am entirely behind all efforts to stop this.

Until fairly recently there was a great deal of pollution in Britain. We remember the London smogs and we enacted legislation to deal with it. Today if a road or railway is being built, care is taken that the surrounding countryside should not be disturbed more than necessary. Chemical emissions from factories are much cleaner than they were. We are concerned about the effect of our activities on wildlife and on the natural environment. Incidentally the so called green option of windmills has a debilitating affect on the environment.

We are keen to enjoy nature as ramblers or observers and for the facilities it provides us for sports of various kinds. In our attitudes to wild animals today, most of us are keen to observe them, rather than shoot them as big game. We enjoy wildlife programmes on television. Some of us are vegetarians or vegans, but that is a choice that some of us make and it in no way constrains the rest of us.

All this concern for nature is to be commended, but the following sections will tell us about a very different phenomenon, disguised by a veneer of concern for the environment.

The dogma of man made global warming

All this fuss about global warming only really emerged as a political phenomenon when other things of more pressing concern were safely out of the way. The industrial revolution had happened and had transformed the economies and living standards of the developed countries. The 2nd World War had been fought and won. The battle against Soviet Communism had been won and the end of the Cold War had been a relatively painless victory for the West. Western politicians thought that they needed new causes to inspire them. They homed in on global warming.

It is essential to distinguish between a reasonable care for the environment and the dogma of man made global warming. The devotees of the latter, whom I shall call the Climatists, are convinced that they are in possession of a truth of overwhelming importance and that the rest of us who are outside their elite circle are miserable sinners. It is no accident that this has come to the fore at a time when in the West the religious certainties of the past are no longer what they once were. At the same time the general Western standard of living is unprecedently high and the most enthusiastic Climatists are rich people.

There is plenty of scientific evidence that there have been tremendous variations of climate in the period of the Earth's existence. There have been ice ages and warm periods. The most recent period of warming was the Medieval Warm period. At that time Southern Greenland was significantly warmer than today. That was well before the Industrial Revolution. Indeed in all these past variations in climate the contribution of man was negligible. It only needs the natural disasters which occur from time to time, such as earthquakes, volcanoes, tsunamis and meteorites hitting the Earth, to show us the enormous power of natural forces uninfluenced by man. In reality the most plausible cause of the variation in the Earth's climate is the activity of the sun. For the science involved, recommended books are "*Unstoppable Every 1500 Years Global Warming*" by Fred Singer and Dennis Avery and "*Heaven And Earth*" by Ian Plimer.

The Climatists believe that the Earth is warming up, though even that is by no means certain. They also assume as an article of faith that because it is warming up the cause must lie in the energy consuming activities of man, rather than in the activities of nature such as the sun. They then go on to assert that we must take every conceivable measure to try and prevent this warming or at least to limit it. They assume arbitrarily that the new conditions produced by the warming would be intolerable for human beings. In fact we do not know whether we should find the new conditions intolerable or not. Furthermore, even if it were possible at great expense to prevent climate change by artificial means, it would still be much better to spend the money on improving the life conditions of the world's poorest. This has been pointed out by Bjorn Lomborg in his book, "*The Sceptical Environmentalist*".

The Climatists give shrill warnings of disasters to be expected from global warming, as is narrated by Steve Goreham in his book, "*Climatism*". There is supposed to be an ocean sea-level rise of 20 feet by the year 2100. In fact sea levels continue to rise at a historic rate of 7 inches per century. In spite of contrary predictions the Earth's icecaps are stable, with the Antarctic icecap growing, the Greenland icecap stable and the Arctic icecap shrinking, but all within the limits of historical variation. Contrary to the predictions of the Climatists, the polar bear is in no danger of becoming extinct. The polar bear population of Nunavut in Canada has increased from 8,000-10,000 fifty years ago to 22,000-25,000 today. Also contrary to their predictions, there is no experimental evidence of a slowing or halting of the Gulf Stream due to man-made global warming (though some fluctuations in the Gulf Stream can be expected). Another disaster predicted is an increase in temperature related deaths. In a study of temperature related deaths in Europe, it was found that deaths due to cold temperatures were nine times greater than those due to hot temperatures. If there is any global warming, the overall prosperity of a country will enable it to cope best with any dangers to health resulting from it. The Climatists always blame every natural disaster on man-made global warming. In fact there have been natural disasters at every period of the Earth's history, but today they tend to be better reported than in the past.

Another dogma of the Climatists is to label carbon dioxide a pollutant. It is not a pollutant. It's presence in the air is necessary for the growth of plants. In so far as it contributes to the greenhouse effect, water vapour also contributes to that. In fact excess carbon dioxide is absorbed in the oceans. Carbon monoxide, sulphur dioxide, nitrogen dioxide and carbon particulates, which are products of incomplete combustion of petrol, are pollutants harmful to people. However, car manufacturers have over the last few decades made every effort to reduce the amount of these in the exhaust of cars. Carbon dioxide is not a pollutant, to treat it as such is bad science. This will be discussed further in the section on the green constraints on industry.

The reliance on renewable energy

The principal forms of renewable energy are hydroelectric, geothermal, solar, wind, tidal and biofuels.

Hydroelectric power is a good source of renewable energy. It operates continuously and gives forth significant amounts of power. It does not need to be supplemented by other forms of energy. It is therefore reliable. However, it is dependant on geography. You cannot create hydroelectric power stations everywhere. Some countries such as Norway make great use of hydroelectric power since the mountainous terrain is suitable. The geographical features of other countries are not.

Geothermal power is similar. In countries such as Iceland, where the terrain is volcanic, geothermal power stations generate significant amounts of power, though some of the geothermal energy is used directly for the heating of buildings. It would not be economic to construct these power stations in areas which are not volcanic.

Solar energy is likely to be more popular in countries closer to the equator than Britain. However, it is not available at night and is much reduced when there is heavy cloud. Though devices to heat water are used, the most popular devices are photovoltaic arrays. In order to obtain significant amounts of energy large areas of land need to be covered with these arrays, thus lessening the amount of land available for agriculture. Often photovoltaic arrays are placed on the roofs of buildings and they may make a contribution to the energy demands of those buildings. However, for significant contributions to the demands of a modern economy, solar power is not a serious contender.

In Britain and the rest of Europe and in America too wind power has hit the headlines. It is popular among green ideologists and is advocated by the EU. However, the wind does not blow all the time and then the turbines are inactive. They are also inactive when the wind is too strong and the turbines have to be shut down. Even when they are working, the amount of energy obtained means that in order to obtain significant amounts large areas of the countryside need to be covered with these structures. Wind power is a low intensity intermittent source of energy.

The intermittent character of wind energy means that any concentration of wind turbines to provide energy has to be backed up with conventional power stations which clock in to provide energy when the turbines are not working. This way of using conventional power stations means that the latter will not be working at maximum efficiency. Paradoxically the installation of wind turbines does not reduce the number of conventional power stations.

Moreover, if wind turbines are situated in the countryside they are apt to kill quite a number of birds. Many people find them unsightly and many areas of natural beauty have been wrecked by them. To construct wind turbines offshore, which has been done quite often, is a big undertaking costing a fair amount of money.

In summary to satisfy the energy demands of a modern economy wind power is not a serious contender. The only thing which makes it at all viable is the vast amount of subsidies it receives.

A certain amount of research has been done on tidal power. One potential advantage of using the tides is that they are regular. Power from this source would not be intermittent, although practical commercial schemes have still to be proposed. Power could be obtained by taking advantage of the

Severn Bore. However, any construction could be opposed as damaging to wildlife.

Sometimes biofuels are considered as a form of renewable energy. Some people feel it to be more acceptable to grow crops to use as fuel rather than to use decayed matter in the form of oil or coal. This is illogical. To grow crops to use as fuel means that there is less land for growing crops for use as food. This is immoral.

Thus hydroelectric power and geothermal power (and possibly tidal power) are perfectly good sources of energy if the geographic features are favourable. Wind power and solar power may have limited applications for remote areas, which have not been connected to the grid. They are totally unsuited to the energy demands of a modern society. The fact is that our energy needs are not predictable and are often unrelated to climatic conditions. Promotion of wind power is due to the blinkered quasi-religious ideology of the green brigade coupled with the greed of businessmen eager to take advantage of the government subsidies.

The green constraints on industry

The Climatist policies of subsidising inefficient and expensive renewables and financially penalising conventional power sources, has resulted in so great a burden on many firms that they have been forced to close down factories or to lay off workers. Also, if a particular factory as part of its operations emits carbon dioxide it is forced to fit costly scrubbers, which can make it uneconomical to continue.

In 2003, largely due to high energy prices, the energy intensive Britannia Zinc works near Bristol was closed with the loss of 400 jobs. In May 2006 it was reported that the UK gas price spike of 2005-2006 had contributed to 6,000 jobs lost over the previous eighteen months in the glass sector. Anglesey Aluminium's plant closed in 2010, following the end of its deal to buy competitively priced electricity from the nearby Wylfa nuclear power station, which had recently passed into state ownership. This was because under EU law to buy from a state owned utility was classified as state aid and was thus deemed illegal. Another of Britain's aluminium plants in Northumberland uses electricity from its own coal fired power station. This will need to be fitted with costly scrubbers to comply with a green directive from the EU. The firm Tata Steel announced the loss of 1,500 jobs in Scunthorpe and Teeside in May 2011 because of rising energy costs.

In *The Daily Mail* of Saturday March 9th 2013, Christopher Booker reported on the conversion of the giant Drax power station in Yorkshire, which is the largest in Britain, from running on coal to running on wood chips. At the moment Drax burns 36,000 tons of coal, brought to its site by 140 coal trains every week and it supplies 7% of all the electricity used in Britain. However, as a result of a change in government policy, triggered by EU rules, Drax will have had to embark on a £700 million switch away from burning coal for which it was designed, in order to convert its six colossal boilers to burn millions of tons of woodchips instead. Most of these chips will come from trees felled in forests covering 4,600 square miles in the USA, from where they will be shipped 3,000 miles across the Atlantic to Britain. Apparently this will save millions of tons of carbon dioxide going into the atmosphere every year. This is a very severe penalty for the denigration of carbon dioxide by the green lobby. Coal is still by far the cheapest means of creating electricity. So the whole exercise will result in a major rise in energy prices. Ironically, Sir David King, formerly the government's chief scientific adviser, is reported to have doubted that, when the full cycle of these wood chips is factored in, there would be any real saving in carbon dioxide emissions at all.

In addition to the rising costs of electricity caused by the adoption of Climatist policies and the impact of these policies on factories engaged in chemical engineering, there is the impact on forms of transport. Cars and lorries suffer greater costs. Trains suffer indirectly. Air travel is directly targeted. All this adds to the costs of industry.

Cars which run completely off batteries have limited mileage before recharging and are uneconomic for ordinary motoring except in cities. Although a certain number of hybrid cars with a battery assisted by petrol have been built, they tend to be expensive. However, use of electric or hybrid vehicles in cities could make sense. For such vehicles to become popular, there would have to a sufficient number of recharging points. Added to this would the ability to re-charge quickly and not to take hours as presently. One thing in favour of such vehicles would be a saving in imported oil, particularly if a much greater proportion of our electricity than it is at present could be obtained from nuclear power stations.

An inevitable result of this adherence to the Climatist ideology is that firms move their operations from Britain to countries where they will not have to endure the high costs. This has already happened and we may expect it to increase if Climatist policies are allowed to continue.

The effects of the climatists on the Third World

China and India are going through their own industrial revolutions. They see their futures as reaching the same economic levels as the already developed nations, and are not paying any attention to green restraints. If they were to do so their economic development would not just be curtailed, but probably made impossible. They are sufficiently large and powerful countries that they can ignore any criticism from the Climatists in the West. The fact that they are going ahead regardless means that actions of Western countries to comply with the Climatist agenda are completely futile. The amount of so-called pollution from the actions of China and India make the green measures of Western countries totally insignificant.

This makes no difference to the determination of the

Climatists to pursue their goal. In their eyes the great thing is to set an example. The smaller undeveloped countries of Africa and Asia are vulnerable as these countries need funding for their development projects. The organisations providing the funds are subject to Climatist pressure, thus there will be no funding for projects unless they comply with the Climatist agenda. For example they are forced to go in for unreliable and unproductive green energy as opposed to conventional energy which could really make a difference. This has resulted in a stranglehold by the Climatists on the economic development of the undeveloped nations of the third world. It is a paradox that a country like Britain gives financial aid to many of these countries while at the same time co-operating in shackling them in furtherance of the Climatist agenda. The aid is to a large extent useless, but the desired economic development which has been thwarted would have been of tremendous benefit.

Nuclear energy and shale gas

Although nuclear energy does not entail the emission into the atmosphere of the biproducts of the combustion of fossil fuels, green ideologists are not comfortable with it. In fact apart from certain well publicised disasters, its safety record is good. The Three Mile Island disaster a few decades ago in the United States, though unfortunate, did not result in any deaths. The Chernobyl disaster in the old Soviet Union was due to the safety of the reactor being not up to Western standards. The recent disaster in Japan shows the folly of building a nuclear reactor in an earthquake zone, incidently the reactor was an old type no longer used in the West. To put things in perspective, we need to remember the numbers of deaths of miners in the past due to the dangers of coal mining, or the tremendous damage to people caused by the disaster at the chemical factory in Bhopal in India. The disposal of nuclear waste has often been cited as a drawback of nuclear energy. However, the methods of disposal used at present seem satisfactory and the potential dangers exaggerated.

What is very much in its favour is that, though the ground covered by a nuclear installation is small, the amount of energy produced is phenomenal. Furthermore, the reactor runs continuously (until it is closed down). Also the amount of fuel used is comparatively small. France has gone down the nuclear route. There is no reason why we should not do the same.

Nuclear energy was something that Britain had a large amount of expertise in. If today more nuclear power stations are built here, I understand that they will be built by a French company. Really it should be a British company which should be doing this employing all those British nuclear specialists together with their expertise.

This paragraph is very much indebted to the article by Lord Nigel Lawson in *The Daily Mail* on Saturday the 8th December 2012. Most of us recognise the vast boon which the discovery of North Sea oil forty years ago brought to the British economy. A new source of energy has come to the fore in the last few years. This is shale gas. Geologists have known about it for some time, but until recently it was not feasible to extract it from the ground. This has changed with the discovery of the process of hydraulic fracturing, called fracking for short. Vast deposits of gas and oil bearing shale have been discovered in the United States and it is estimated that that country will overtake Saudi Arabia as the world's largest oil producer in 2017, in consequence it will virtually cease to import any. Similar shale deposits are located throughout the world including Europe and particularly in Britain. The first large discovery to be explored in this country is the Bowland shale under the Blackpool area of Lancashire. This turns out to be a thicker seam than any in the United States. The company behind the exploration has announced that Blackpool may be sitting on one of the biggest shale fields in the world, with a reserve of 200 trillion cubic feet lying under the Lancashire countryside. That is enough to keep the UK going for 50 years and create 5,000 more jobs. There are other shale deposits in other parts of Britain too. This proves that the notion that the world will run out of fossil fuels in the foreseeable future is not true.

The advent of shale gas transforms the energy situation. No longer will the West and Britain in particular be dependant on the Middle East or on Russia. If used rightly it will assist the regeneration of manufacturing industry in addition to helping out with the national debt. Predictably the green lobby are not enthusiastic about the advent of shale gas. However, in his Autumn 2012 statement the Chancellor George Osborne announced a new gas strategy designed to promote the fastest practicable exploitation of the UK's shale gas deposits. This is very much to be welcomed.

We need to embrace both nuclear energy and shale gas. If we do, prosperity is on the horizon. If we do not, we will certainly have problems.

The energy way forward

Due to the Climatist ideology, backed up by the EU, we are supposed to shut down our coal fired power stations, in order to curb our Carbon footprint. This is an absurd example of gesture politics. Whatever we do makes no difference, owing to the activities of China and India, who are busy industrialising with little reference to green constraints. We should certainly not close down any coal fired power stations until we have reliable energy replacements. If the government and the EU were not in favour of it, we would not be closing them down at all. Furthermore, all but one of our nine nuclear power stations are due to be closed by 2023. However, the French company EDF energy has just been granted planning permission to build a new nuclear station at Hinckley Point.

The fact that North Sea oil is not in fact running out with new fields having been discovered is certainly welcome. The discovery of shale gas in Britain, which is now recoverable by the method of fracking, is a cause for rejoicing. It is good news that the Chancellor has backed the exploitation of shale gas, against the luke-warm attitudes of the green brigade. Nevertheless our nuclear power stations must be replaced, as nuclear energy can make an enormous contribution to our energy requirements with virtually no snags attached to it.

We need to be severely practical in our energy policy, with green hang-ups resolutely kicked into the long grass. Any shortage of energy could lead to electricity blackouts and energy rationing, or could result in Britain being faced with importing a great part of its energy requirements. This would put us at the mercy of price rises in an energy hungry world and also at the mercy of governments in the most unstable parts of the world (Latin America, the Middle East and Russia).

It is true that we could reduce our energy requirements to some extent by more extensive insulation of buildings and private houses. Also devices which use energy could become more efficient by improved technology, as they have in the past (e.g. computers are much smaller and more efficient and use less energy than they did in the past). Nevertheless this can only make an important but minor contribution to our needs.

Climatists need to be viewed as enemies to be combated. If they have their way they will reduce Britain to economic ruin and will make any measures to improve the lot of its citizens impossible. We must understand that the prime victims of electricity blackouts and rises in energy prices, apart from industry, are the poor and underprivileged of our society. Climatism is a war of well-healed greens against not so well-healed ordinary people. We must realise that the Climatists operate as fanatics. Instead of regarding critics of the Climatist ideology as honourable opponents, they portray them as enemies of humanity.

The Climatists do not behave in a scientific manner. David Bellamy has not been invited to do programmes on the BBC, since he expressed disagreement with the Climatist ideology.

For further information about this, the books, "*Climatism*" by Steve Goreham and "*Watermelons*" by James Delingpole, are of great interest.

We must insist that the existence of secure energy supplies come before any green considerations, whether promoted by the EU or by our local Climatists. The department of Energy and Climate Change must be renamed the department of Energy. We must abolish all subsidies to renewable energy. Then we can have a sensible energy policy, based on nuclear power and fossil fuels including shale gas. We must cancel all regulations on industry due to Climatist influence, and should only put in place regulations demanded by common sense for genuine science rather than ideology. To be able to do all this, we should firstly take Britain out of the EU, so that we would not be subject to their interference. This would be an integral part of our attempts to resurrect British industry and make a start with a new politics for our country.

5

Britain and the EU

There was idealism behind the EU, but it was based on a misreading of history and a lack of understanding of the concept of the nation state.

There was the feeling that the history of Europe has been full of wars between the various nations, with the 1st and 2nd World Wars being the most recent and being particularly bloody and all embracing. What is ignored is that all these wars have been due to one or other nation trying to exercise hegemony over its neighbours. They were not nationalist wars but imperialist wars. England was prevented from exercising hegemony over France and Scotland in the Middle Ages and has never tried to do so since. From that time on we have had the Catholic Church, Spain, Turkey under the Ottomans, France under the Bourbons, France under Napoleon, Germany under the Kaiser, Germany under Hitler, Russia under the Tsars and Russia under the Bolsheviks, all of them trying to exercise hegemony over their neighbours. This has been the cause of the various wars (including the Cold War), not the national aspirations of any individual nation state.

It is very important to get this right. If aggressor nations had decided not to attack, there would have been no wars.

Some say that if we were all the same and national differences did not exist, there would be no wars. This is a futile argument. It is like saying that, if there were no differences between human beings, there would be no conflicts between them. As a matter of fact it is not true. People who resemble each other in most respects can still quarrel. Besides trying to make all nations the same would be obnoxious.

Europe is tremendously enriched by the differences between its component nations.

After the 2nd World War the superpower hegemony which European nations had possessed over the rest of the world was replaced by that of nations outside Europe. It would become increasingly suicidal for any European nation to go to war with its neighbours. Increase in inter-European tourism meant that there was a decrease in any inclination to do so. As for threats against Western Europe from outside, namely from Russia, that was taken care of by the formation of NATO and by the American nuclear umbrella. It was NATO and America which have preserved the peace in the latter part of the 20th century, not the formation of the EU, which has been an irrelevance.

There may have been advantages for some countries to form a trade pact, which was what the EU was originally thought to be. In the case of Britain the advantages were few, if any, since the EU contained Britain's competitors. But it was totally unnecessary to form a European superstate, which was from the start the intention of the real Euro-enthusiasts such as Jean Monnet. The only people who would actually benefit from this would be the EU bureaucrats and some politicians who would like to posture on an international stage. The EU is undemocratic. Since it is formed of a collection of disparate peoples, with economic, political and cultural differences, it could hardly be anything else. The present troubles of the EU, particularly in relation to the eurozone (the collection of countries in the single currency), could have been predicted. One size does not fit all and if you try and force it to do so you are in trouble.

Some enthusiasts are ambitious for the EU to become a superpower to rival the United States, Russia and China. This is just imperialistic posturing. It is totally unnecessary. For defence purposes, a military alliance between European countries such as NATO, is all that is required.

Some people have at the back of their minds the idea of the EU as a means of constraining Germany. However, if Germany behaves as a good neighbour, there is no problem, even if she happens to be the most economically prosperous of the European states. If she were to decide not to behave as a good neighbour and that seems very unlikely, then joint membership of the EU would be no protection.

To sum up the nations of Europe need to rediscover the freedoms and advantages of the nation state, which nations outside Europe have learned to cherish.

Britain's fear of being independent

Britain's application to join the Common Market, which became the EU, came at a time when her political class was suffering from a loss of confidence. It seemed to many of them that Britain had escaped from disaster and had emerged victorious in the 2nd World War by the skin of her teeth. The reasons for the near disaster were not properly understood. The post war situation where the country was faced with an inevitable loss of empire seemed to many to present her with a prospect of isolation at severely reduced strength. There was also the fact that politicians and commanders who had participated as equals in decisions of global importance in the war. were afterwards reduced to a less prestigious role. The fact that Britain seemed to be doing less well economically than her European competitors strengthened this psychology of gloom.

The near escape from disaster in 1940 can be understood by bearing in mind two things. The first was that in the period between 1918 and 1939 Britain was severely overstretched with commitments greater than she had ever had in the past. Never before that time had she been responsible both for Eastern and Central Europe and for most of the Middle East in addition to her own empire. Secondly she failed to realise that in this precarious situation the League of Nations in

Geneva was useless, and that it was necessary for her to maintain a very high level of defence preparedness. As a matter of fact, Hitler could have been stopped without the danger of war when he sent his troops into the Rhineland against the stipulations of the Treaty of Versailles. After that time it was more dangerous. The situation after 1945 was completely different. The American alliance and the formation of NATO made her defence situation much more secure in spite of the Soviet threat. She was no longer alone.

The empire in its declining years should have been regarded more as a liability than an asset. The grant of independence to the various components of the empire in the post war years should have been thought of as the lifting of burdens of responsibility. It did not in fact indicate any reduction in Britain's actual power in the world, she was still a power of medium rank. However, joining the Common Market, which later became the EU, was effectively joining an empire in the making as a constituent part.

Increasingly in this post war world Britain was less successful than her competitors, but the cure for this predicament was up to her. No amount of joining up with other countries was going to help. Either Britain managed to improve her economic position by her own efforts, or her position would remain the same or get worse.

What is the position of Britain today? Membership of the EU has been damaging. The situation as regards defence is perfectly secure provided she retains a reasonable defence capability. Her overseas commitments, provided she does not artificially increase them, have become very small, being no greater than those of other European countries.

We can conclude that Britain should have no fear of leaving the EU and taking up her destiny as an independent nation. The mood of her political elite when she decided to join the Common Market could be described as a case of unjustified fright. Her situation, though difficult, was not desperate and there was nothing that intelligence, resolution and application could not have put right.

Britain unable to be protectionist

As members of the EU Britain is not supposed to give preference in employment or in any other fields to our own citizens over citizens of other EU countries who are resident here. Furthermore, we are not supposed to give preference in contracts to British firms above firms of other EU countries.

I strongly suspect that, in spite of both being members of the EU, the French and the Germans would give preference to their own firms as regards contracts and to their own citizens as regards employment. Britain, throughout the period it has been a member, has been more assiduous in adhering to EU regulations than any other member. Many people have told me that other countries throughout the world look after their own interests, their own firms and their own citizens better than we do.

The attitude of governments of either party and many public authorities in Britain seems to be that cost is all that matters. They are disinclined to be patriotic. Membership of the EU gives these people a perfect cover for their behaviour. They can always say that the EU forbids them to act in a patriotic manner, whether it does or not. However, protectionist policies, especially if enshrined in law, would be impossible for Britain to pursue while it was inside the EU. This is an additional reason for leaving.

Costs to Britain

For this section I am indebted to the pamphlet by Tim Congdon, "*How Much Does The European Union Cost Britain?*". He estimates that Britain is roughly 10% of GDP, about £150 billion, worse off every year through being a member of the EU.

This figure is made up as follows:

(1) The direct fiscal cost, consisting of gross payments to EU institutions. This is 1% of GDP.

(2) The costs of complying with EU regulations. This is 5% of GDP.

(3) The costs of resource misallocation caused by the CAP among other things. This adds up to 3.25% of GDP.

(4) The cost of lost jobs. The Open British labour market from 2004 allowed 700,000 Eastern Europeans into Britain, taking away the jobs of over 100,000 people born in the UK. This is 0.25% of GDP.

(5) The costs of waste, fraud and corruption. This includes the throwing back into the sea of fish as demanded by the Common Fisheries Policy. It also includes the waste of over prescriptive water standards. The total costs of all this are 0.25% of GDP.

(6) Contingent liabilities such as the costs of benefits tourism. This adds up to 0.25% of GDP.

If we remain in the EU, we can expect to incur further costs, since the EU is forever seeking to increase its control over its members. The EU also has designs on the City of London. Furthermore, the present crisis in the Eurozone has resulted in many demands to us from the EU for help in the bailouts of the weaker members.

If we are thinking of saving money, leaving the EU must come top of the list.

Infringement of British democracy

It has been said that 70% of our legislation comes from the EU. Even when our parliament is able to scrutinise this legislation, it has no power to reject it or any part of it. This legislation concerns the various regulations which the EU decides to implement regarding the various goods produced and services given in Britain. The EU will have a bright idea about something and after a certain amount of bargaining, it will decide to implement it as a regulation. The bargaining will consist of Britain allowing some other country to have its way in one area, in exchange for Britain having its way in another area. This is a far cry from a proper scrutiny of a particular issue, which is what we expected our parliament to conduct in the past. Additional damage results from our civil servants gold plating regulations coming from the EU so that they are more stringent than they need be. Other countries in the EU do not do this. Also on occasions other countries get away with not applying EU regulations if it is against their interest to do so. Most of these EU regulations cost Britain a fair sum of money.

Big corporations are sufficiently rich and powerful that they can successfully lobby EU officials so that the regulations proposed are not too damaging to them. Small businesses by contrast do not have the resources to do this.

There is also the existence of the European Arrest Warrant, which allows British citizens to be arrested and carted off to other EU member states for offences alleged to have been committed in those states. This occurs without reference to British courts, who are powerless to prevent it. This has already happened to a number of British citizens. This state of affairs is made worse by the fact that the justice systems of many member states leave much to be desired. This is a direct attack on commonly assumed British rights to justice. This is described in detail in the pamphlet of Gerald Batten, entitled "*Freedom, Security and Justice?*". It is an excellent pamphlet and is essential reading for anybody who cares about British justice. It should be noted that the only way to escape from this is by Britain leaving the EU.

Of course there are areas such as the budget or control of interest rates, or other matters which the EU has not yet brought within its orbit where Britain still has control. Nobody should assume that the present situation is permanent, since the long term aim of the EU is to bring all areas of politics under its control. The end of the road, if our presence in the EU is allowed to continue, would see our Westminster parliament reduced to the status of a county council.

We may conclude that our political class is no longer interested in particular issues as such. Possibly they are just interested in the trappings of power and the prestige which goes with it. Perhaps bargaining comes naturally to them. Most of our politicians today are less affected by what is happening than the people who elect them.

Thus Britain today is less of a democracy than most people think it is, chiefly because of our membership of the EU, but also because of the unrepresentative character of our political class, which needs a moral and political refurbishment.

Immigration and climatist policies

With regard to immigration the EU allows free movement of citizens of EU states throughout the union. Some countries obtained relief from having to implement this immediately, when some of the Eastern block members joined in the recent past. Britain did not take advantage of this provision, with the result that the influx of people from these states was much greater than the politicians predicted. With regard to the immigration of citizens of other EU states we are forced to admit them as long as we are in the EU. That means that as more states join the EU, their citizens have the right to come here and obtain British benefits. (These benefits in many cases even allow them to claim for children living in their country of origin.) This puts additional strain on our social services and it is not helped by the fact that many of these migrants have a weak knowledge of English. With regard to immigrants from other parts of the world the European Court of Human Rights, to which we belong, has frequently prevented us from deporting people, however undesirable they have been, because of concern about the treatment they would receive on arrival at their destinations. In reality if we want to have full control of our borders we must take Britain out of the EU.

The Climatist policies which we have put into place are the results of the attitudes of our own political class as well as of our membership of the EU. The EU has set forth certain Climatist objectives to be followed by all the member states. Britain has chosen to abide by these and even to surpass them. Quite frankly we need not have built as many wind farms as we have. If we did manage to convert our political class to the folly of carrying out Climatist policies, we would then have to leave the EU to be free to embark on our own convictions.

The European Court of Human Rights

The European Court of Human Rights in Strasbourg, in spite of being set up as a protector of civilisation, has become a protector of terrorists and criminals.

In a recent case two Muslim terrorists have launched a legal bid to have their convictions in the British courts overturned by Strasbourg on human rights grounds. Salahuddin Amin was given a life sentence in 2007 for his part in a plot to cause carnage in the South East of England by detonating a massive bomb filled with ammonium nitrate. Rangzieb Ahmed was a senior member of the Al Qaeda global terror network, acting as the linkman between operatives in Britain and their commanders abroad. He too was given a life sentence. They are appealing to Strasbourg, as they claim that their rights were infringed because the British authorities, in collecting evidence against them, colluded in their torture by the Pakistani security services. This allegation has already been addressed by the British courts and thrown out. However the officials at Strasbourg have decided that the application from these two men can proceed.

In another case the court in Strasbourg blocked the deportation to Jordan of Abu Qatada to face terrorism charges, a legal farce which has already cost the British taxpayer over £3 million. Twelve years after his original arrest he is still in the UK costing the taxpayer ever greater sums of money.

We have just been given permission in 2012 by the Court in Strasbourg to deport Abu Hamza to the United States, where he is accused of planning a terror training camp and of assisting hostage takers in the Yemen. A decade ago he was preaching anti-British hate as iman of the Finsbury Park mosque. He was originally arrested in August 2004 and it has taken eight years before we were finally allowed to deport him.

These are just three examples of the dubious actions of the European Court of Human Rights in Strasbourg. It should be noted that this court contains judges from places such as Russia, Azerbaijan and Serbia, which have nothing like the British record of fairness.

EU legislation is thought to have prevented the removal of around 5,000 foreign criminals from Britain, many of them on the grounds that they have "a right to a family life" under Article 8 of the Convention on Human Rights, having started a relationship or fathered children here. Also the court in Strasbourg demands that the British Government gives the vote to prisoners, against the wishes of the British people and against the wishes of our own parliament.

Realising what a damaging institution the court in Strasbourg has become and that all it does is to provide a good living to cynical lawyers and left wing ideologies, Britain should leave the court and refuse to accept its jurisdiction.

What if Britain leaves?

If Britain left the EU, the EU would lose the British contribution to the budget. This would be a bit of a loss, since Britain is one of the richer countries and gives to the EU much more than it receives back. It would mean a greater burden on the wealthier countries remaining and increasingly on Germany.

Whether the EU could continue to exist, if Britain left, is a problem for the remaining members. I think it could, but our departure would give it a bit of a jolt. The EU does not want us to leave but there is nothing that the EU could do to prevent it. There is no viable economic retaliation which the EU could make, since we import significantly more from EU countries than we export to them.

Possibly the EU might be quite happy for us to leave since, in spite of losing our financial contribution, it would make it easier for it to pursue its federalist dreams.

Leaving the EU would save Britain a considerable amount of money and would have the potential for a resurrection of British democracy. Once out of the EU, the government in power and the political establishment as a whole would have nobody to blame but themselves, if things did not go as well as they wanted. The electorate would know that all political decisions affecting their lives would depend upon the members of parliament whom they elected and whom they had the power to dismiss at the next election.

At present the money which the EU returns to us as grants (in spite of being far less than we give them) is spent on projects chosen by the EU. Leaving the EU would mean that we spent whatever sums of money we chose on what we wanted to spend it on. Coping with the present financial situation would be made significantly easier. The government would not have to carry out such large cuts in expenditure as at present. Leaving the EU could also result in far more jobs for UK citizens, since apart from anything else they would no longer have to face competition from the citizens of other EU states.

We would hope that Britain would play a constructive part in the world. Our defence should be maintained at reasonable strength and we should continue our membership of NATO which has given us good value. Outside the EU, we would be able to give the poor countries of Africa and elsewhere more favourable terms of trade than before. With regard to the other countries in the EU whose ranks we would have left, I have no doubt that after the dust had settled, our relations with them would be perfectly amicable. We should emphasise that our objections are simply to the EU. The UK has no quarrel with the peoples of Europe or their countries but wish to be friends with them.

6

Reflections on Politics Today

The 2012 Olympics and Paralympics

I am among a vast number of people to be enthralled and inspired by the London Olympics and Paralympics of 2012. All parts of Great Britain entered into the spirit of the games in their enthusiasm. They can justly be considered a great success.

I was glad about the great success of the athletes of team GB. All the athletes demonstrated the can do spirit in full measure. Whether or not they won, they showed that it was desirable to win. They had already won contests to participate. Not for them was the opinion that things were impossible. They understood the gruelling training that competing in the games entailed, but in spite of that they chose to do so.

The games were about genuine achievement. There was no cheating in the games and apart from a few episodes in the past, where some athletes have used stamina enhancing drugs, there has been no cheating in previous Olympic games either. This made the games an island of genuine achievement in a world where so much mediocrity prevails.

In the years leading up to the games a great many of the playing fields of state schools have been sold off. This is terrible. Are we to rely solely on the youngsters from independent schools to be the athletes of the future? It is not surprising that many of the nation's youngsters are in danger of becoming obese. The true message of the games is that this selling off of school playing fields must stop and indeed be reversed. This alone can justify the expense of staging the games in London. Every child should have the opportunity to take part in and enjoy sport and games.

The message from the Paralympics greatly backs up the message from the Olympics, but it has a profound message of its own. It has taught us to look at people for what they can do rather than for what they can't do. It has shown us that, though disabled, the Paralympic athletes were superb athletes in absolute terms. It has told us something essential about human beings, that they want not to be pitied but to achieve.

How many people do we regard in one way or another as objects of care in our society? We should really look at these people in a new light. Certainly we should help people in practical ways. The object of such help should be just that and not to provide a professional occupation for helpers. Both the Olympic and the Paralympic athletes received such help. We should at all times attempt to instill in people the conviction that success is possible and the desire to strive through thick and thin to attain it.

Reflections on political correctness

Two things need to be very sharply distinguished, common humanity and political correctness. The latter pretends to be nothing more than common humanity. That is not true. Common humanity contains an element of discrimination. Not everyone is a proper subject of compassion or is deserving of friendship and help. Being well disposed towards everyone regardless of their behaviour makes a mockery of the concept of common humanity. A person displaying common humanity would support someone deserving of help even if all the world was hostile. Political correctness would never do that. Indeed the latter is really just a matter of obeying rules. It is a modern form of etiquette. It is very convenient and does not require anyone to give serious thought to anything at all. Political correctness is really conformity plus a desire to present a good image.

When does political correctness come into play? Is it when a particular injustice occurs but is not recognised as such? No. Is it when it is a matter of dispute whether something is a particular injustice or not? No. Political correctness comes into play when matters are more or less settled. Political correctness does not correct any of the injustices of society and it never has fulfilled that role. It supposedly ensures that nobody is offended, rather in the way that good table manners is helpful on social occasions.

The sanction against offending people is often extended to ensure no criticism is made against certain people, however, deserved such criticism may be.

There is an alternative to a society governed by political correctness. That is a society where controversy is accepted as part of life and that it is up to each individual to form their own opinion. Such a world is a bit frightening to some. They are afraid of making their own judgements, but that is what people must do, if they are to take their place as free citizens in a free country.

Political correctness stifles debate and enforces conformity. If it persists long enough, what has been kept under wraps by it bursts forth with insurrectionary vigour and violence. The end result of a reign of political correctness could be that it dramatically fails to prevent the occurrence of what it purports to fear. It latches on to one of our great virtues, our common humanity, distorts it and becomes one of the most damaging things that our country has ever had to face. We must declare loud and clear that we value common humanity greatly, but are diametrically opposed to political correctness.

Pseudo-liberalism

According to pseudo-liberalism it is not permissible to say that one culture, civilisation, or set of behaviours is superior to that of another. That is said to be a relic of Victorian times and an example of cultural imperialism. It is not even permissible to say that the traditional British culture or set of behaviour is more suited to this country. Even though some bits of behaviour of certain ethnic groups are totally opposed to our mores, it is not permissible to criticise persons behaving in these ways or to suggest that the people in question might fit in better in their countries of origin. Further it is considered racialist or zenophobic to say that immigrants may be displacing the indigenous population from the market for jobs and housing.

There is a refusal to judge people, a wish to be impartial and a desire to be untarnished by worldly squabbles. In general a reluctance to be moralistic, perhaps out of a fear that the conduct of themselves or their friends might be subject to criticism. There is also an ideal of pseudo-scientific objectivity. pseudo-liberals despise and do not understand the world of politics. They therefore cherish the illusion of bringing the uninvolved and unemotional atmosphere of science into the controversies of people, where frankly it is not appropriate.

Another important ingredient of the pseudo-liberal package is a hostility to patriotism and to the existence of the nation state. This is partly the result of these people priding themselves on being ever so intellectual, and therefore not subject to normal partisan emotions. In their view no particular nation is any more responsible for aggression than any other. Those of them who were Communists had a bit of an intellectual difficulty with this in the 2nd World War, when the Soviet Union was attacked in 1941. They got round it, since for them the Soviet Union was a rather special kind of nation state. It is very convenient for them that there have sometimes been wars between nation states. They use this fact in their propaganda, despite the fact that there have been much longer periods when countries have been at peace. The idea of a country having a particular history and culture and consisting of citizens who are part of all this cuts no ice with the pseudo-liberals. As far as they are concerned, a person is just an entity who ticks the boxes of the forms required to be filled in for statutory purposes. Therefore, a country is of no more significance than a hotel or a camping site.

The planet Earth is popular with the pseudo-liberals. It is above our mundane worldly concerns. In their eyes the individual is of no consequence compared with the magnitude of the universe. It also satisfies their hostility to the Industrial Revolution to be able to harness the planet against industrial activities. They delight in saying it is our fault that allegedly the poor planet has been damaged by us. Caring for the planet is regarded by the politically correct as supremely virtuous, in addition to being much in favour with the bureaucrats of the EU.

Behind the adherence of many people to pseudo-liberal ideas there is a wish to be virtuous. Christianity is influential here. There is a desire to do the virtuous thing even though nobody else is doing it. There is the desire to do something even though your action results in the opposite to what you desire. To these people motivation is all important regardless of the consequences.

Some people have put another interpretation on the mixture of policies I have assembled under the label of pseudo-liberalism. They have suggested that just as the Marxist left attempted to transform society by radically altering its economic system, the pseudo-liberals are trying to transform society by radically altering its cultural bases. Thus they are latter day Marxists who, having concluded that their first policy of radically altering the economics of society has failed, now think that their second policy stands a chance of success. Whether desires of this kind motivate the pseudo-liberals I do not know. I think it motivates some of them. What it does mean is that we who are opposed to the pseudo-liberals must act to combat them as if we believed that they were working to a plan.

Behaviour of the two main parties in recent times

The Labour governments of Blair and Brown accepted the economic landscape left by Thatcherism. They deleted Clause Four from the Labour Party's constitution. They were enthusiastic about service industries and about the activities of the City of London. They relied upon the latter to sustain the economy. Like the Conservatives before them, they did not question the sophisticated wrapping up of unsecured debt to finance their expenditure. They did not display any great concern for manufacturing industry, even though the displaced workers were their natural constituency. Further their allowance of unrestricted mass immigration was extremely damaging to the interests of the latter.

The Blair and Brown governments seemed particularly inthralled to the ideals of pseudo-liberalism. These appeared almost to have replaced their loyalties to their natural constituency, which was in many ways put on one side and neglected. They thought that the latter would continue to vote for them come what may and that to give themselves a majority, they had to seek the new pastures of the new immigrants and the metropolitan elite.

The pseudo-liberal policies were unrestricted mass immigration, enthusiasm for staying in the EU and complying with its regulations. A desire to increase our overseas aid contribution, enthusiastic adoption of green policies advocated by the climatist lobby together with its reliance on renewable energy. Plus, the going ahead with devolution with its risks for the unity of the country. The sole exception to the pursuit of this agenda was Gordon Brown's prevention of Britain's adoption of the Euro.

The Conservative opposition made no real protest against the mass immigration permitted by the Blair government, nor did it go against the green Climatist agenda or the money spent on overseas aid. There was some euroscepticism from the Conservative ranks, but it was not adopted by the leaders of the party. This was despite the unpopularity of these pseudo-liberal policies with conservative voters. The true reasons for the Conservatives being perceived as the nasty party, were the adverse affects of their monetarist policies on industry rather than the opposition of most Conservatives to the pseudo-liberal agenda. Under Mrs Thatcher, many British companies went to the wall and very many jobs were lost, with its debilitating effect on many communities. The Conservative party under Cameron showed no understanding of this and instead tried to win over the metropolitan intellectual elite. For an understanding of the present leadership of the Conservative party, the book, "*The Cameron Delusion*", by Peter Hitchens is illuminating, as is the book by Peter Oborne, "*The Triumph Of The Political Class*". The present leadership of the Conservative party is divorced from its supporters in the country who continue to vote for it, though in diminishing numbers, out of a mixture of tribal loyalty and inertia.

Some do well out of things as they are

Some people are rich enough or privileged enough to be unaffected by the strains imposed on the social services or the housing market by mass immigration. They may live in expensive areas unaffected by crime and with satisfactory schools. If necessary they can go private in their needs for health or education. They may like the ability to hire immigrant labour to do various jobs for them and can pay them less than they would have to pay the natives. Such people can also do quite well out of the EU. The EU pays its officials quite handsomely and loyalty to the EU cause is definitely rewarded. The grants of money to overseas aid do not worry them. They may be members of organisations managing the aid and visiting other parts of the world to distribute it. The climatist agenda does not worry them either. Some of them may have become richer by allowing the erection of wind turbines on their land. With government subsidies behind green energy projects, there is money to be made in going along with it.

When we think of the sale of British industry, there were shareholders who benefited, as well as executives who received golden handshakes. The banks have been very much in the news lately and we have learned of the lavish handouts to bankers when the bank is doing badly, just as much as when it is doing well. Our politicians have not as much control over our country as they once had, but that has made no difference to the remuneration they receive. Our local authorities may shut down public libraries and sell off school playing fields, but council executives seem to be doing quite well financially.

We live in a world where with honourable exceptions the accepted goal is to get rich whether one has made a genuine contribution to the welfare of people or not. In this situation it is perhaps invidious to single out particular groups of people to blame. What is needed is a change of acceptable behaviour right across the board.

Patriotism

Patriotism has many associations. Some people were ever so keen on being patriotic in the days when Britain was a superpower, when she had an empire upon which the sun never set and when she was the workshop of the world. They were also patriotic in the first and second world wars. In those days personal ambition and patriotism walked hand in hand. Of course in the two world wars a deeper patriotism, a true love of Britain and its civilisation, was widespread among all sections of the population. However, in the decades since the second world war, when Britain suffered a decline in power, in status and in economic performance, the fair weather patriots were less patriotic than before.

In spite of the relative decline of Britain in power, she along with all developed countries experienced a great increase in prosperity in the latter part of the 20th century. This spread to almost all parts of the population. With this increase in prosperity, patriotism along with other old moral values suffered a decline.

We do have reasons to be proud of our country. There are

things to be proud of both in our past and in our present. We also have certain values which are dear to the majority of our people. There are a variety of freedoms which we enjoy today which are the results of long struggles throughout our history. Apart from feelings of national pride, true patriotism is a feeling of loyalty and affection for one's country because it is one's own. The majority of our people have feelings of this nature about the country, which are deep rooted and come to the fore especially when the concept of patriotism appears to be under attack.

The maintenance of the union

The responsibility for the establishment of the devolved assemblies in Scotland and Wales rests with all three parties. If our politicians had been keener to avoid this and had been willing to make the necessary sacrifices, then perhaps things might have been different. The existence of the devolved assemblies can be borne with equanimity, provided the union of Britain as one country is preserved. After all they can be regarded in the same light as the existence of the separate state legislatures in the United States. The union of the states as one country is preserved. The wealth and political strength of the United States would be considerably diminished if some of the states decided to separate.

Similarly the economic and political strength of Britain would be very severely reduced if Scotland decides to become a separate country. For defence purposes Britain is much stronger as one country and Scotland itself would become poorer without the financial support of the UK treasury.

Many of us are wise enough to recognise the truths I have enunciated in the last paragraph. So are a number of countries and organisations which do not hold our interests at heart, but wish to reduce the strength which a united Britain has.

At present Britain is important enough both actually and

potentially for hostile powers to desire to put us out of the gameplay. A united Britain was a firm supporter of NATO and was apart from France the sole nuclear power in Europe. That supplied a strong motive for a Soviet desire to damage us. Today Britain is known to have the most eurosceptic population of all the member states of the EU. The EU would have a strong motive for wanting to reduce British power. Other powers in the world today may also have reasons for desiring to do this. It is very important that, when thinking about the union, we should recognise that some foreigners have a vested interest in wishing to terminate it. Some of our own intellectuals would not mind if that happened either.

I am convinced that united we are immeasurably stronger in every way, economically and politically, than divided. The maintenance of the union requires responsible people in all parts of Britain to do their utmost to preserve it. The 2012 Olympics and Paralympics, in which athletes from all parts of Britain excelled may have helped. In short let us as a prime undertaking work to preserve Britain as one country.

A political realignment and first things first

The really important matters in politics today are the following:

(a) Britain leaving the EU

(b) Curbing and to an extent reversing mass immigration

(c) Ending overseas aid wholly or partially

(d) Stopping the reliance on renewable energy and stopping the Climatist inspired industrial regulations

(e) Preserving the unity of Britain as one country and

(f) Doing everything possible for the resurrection of British manufacturing industry.

These policies have an appeal to many politicians both Labour and Conservative. At present they do not appeal to the front bench politicians of either party. If they did so appeal, we would not be in the mess we are in today. However, they will appeal to a significant number of politicians from both parties and to a majority of their supporters in the country. As distinct from these policies being extremist, sixty years ago almost all politicians, both Conservative and Labour, would have agreed with them.

Conservative and Labour politicians who are in favour of these policies together with politicians from the United Kingdom Independence Party should get together to campaign for them as one block. In this ad hoc association both Conservative and Labour politicians need to be careful about the political susceptibilities of the other. If this gathering of people should come about, it should be clear that what unites them is much more important than what divides them. Only after these policies which I have put forward have been implemented will it be possible to return to normal politics. Further, unless these policies are implemented, it will not be possible for the adherents of either party to do what their supporters desire.

There is a lot of talk at the present time of the need for cuts in public expenditure and there are moves to do this in the conventional way by cutting benefits. There are arguments in favour of the latter, but we should postpone any moves to do this until we have accomplished the above primary objectives. The benefits system is complicated. The whole thing needs to be looked at, not in the light of how much it costs, but on which benefits are necessary to help people and which just foster a dependency situation. Any reform needs a lot of discussion with people who know the situation at the grass roots. The philosophy should be that the state is very willing to pay for things which actually do good, but not willing to pay for anything which does not.

There are other measures which would elicit almost universal approval:

(a) The reinstatement of discipline in many of Britain's state schools. This would benefit most disadvantaged children. The better off can ensure that their children go to schools where this is less of a problem.

(b) The restoration of law and order in many neighbourhoods by the policy of having "bobbies on the beat" and cutting down on the red tape hampering police forces today. This would benefit the less privileged part of the population most in particular.

(c) There have been a number of cases where the law abiding citizen has been arrested rather than the person who was committing a criminal offense. Reversal of this trend would be highly desirable.

(d) The forbidding of the sale of public libraries which has been unfortunately happening recently. We must give every encouragement to literacy. The forbidding of the sale of school playing fields.

Such things as gay marriage and House of Lords reform should be consigned to the scrap heap. These kinds of things are what you think about when you have nothing better to do. This is all about presenting a certain image and has no connection with what is good or necessary for the country.

The fanaticism of our foes

Normally with political opponents we assume that their different viewpoints and policies are the reflection of the interests which they represent. The enthusiasts for the EU, for mass immigration, for overseas aid, or for the Climatist agenda do not really represent hard economic interests in the country. They represent enthusiasts for a particular idea. At bottom their campaigning stance and popular appeal is weak, so they enhance it by artificial means.

That is why they portray people who disagree with them as extremists. Those who are unhappy with our membership of the EU are portrayed as zenophobes or extreme nationalists.

Opponents to mass immigration are depicted as racists and zenophobes. While those who object to overseas aid are regarded as lacking in compassion for the world's poorest. Anyone who disagree with the Climatist creed of man made global warming and of trying to reverse it by vigorous action, are referred to as climate change deniers, as if they were Neanderthal believers in a flat Earth. People who disagree with these enthusiasts are not treated as honourable opponents, but are looked upon as beyond the pale. Another label they give to their opponents is that they are very right wing. This is quite false. It is they who are elitist and we who are on the side of ordinary people.

These people try to prevent open discussion of the issues. They are not above playing about with evidence and using any economic or political power they have. Hence there was the fraudulent hockey stick graph to promote the thesis of man made global warming. Scientists who dissent from the thesis have been threatened professionally. The phenomenon of mass immigration was kept under wraps while it was happening, but was brought into the open by the whistleblower, Steve Moxon, in his book "*The Great Immigration Scandal*". The realities of our overseas aid have been reported by hard hitting journalists. Our involvement with the EU has only been brought to the public eye by eurosceptic organisations and by the electoral challenge of the United Kingdom Independence Party.

On all four issues the leaderships of the three main political parties are fellow travellers with these ideologies. Ordinary scrutiny of ideas seems to have gone out of the window, making it imperative for the rest of us to steadfastly oppose them.

The political scene today

One important factor behind the political scene today, is that in the last sixty years there have been an awful lot of changes in peoples' lives and in how they look at things. There have been the technological changes, the political changes and the changes in attitudes and customs. There have been too many for them to digest in this relatively short time. They have possibly succeeded in having decided opinions about only a few of the issues that crop up. Therefore, very many things have happened, regardless of what the public thought about them one way or the other.

In Peter Oborne's book "*The Triumph Of The Political Class*" he describes the evolution in recent years of politicians as a class apart from the rest of society, who have more in common with each other, regardless of which party they belong to, than with the rest of society. It was not like this in the past. Then the vast majority of them had definite roots in particular sections of the population. At that time too, there was more division between the parties regarding their approach to issues of contention.

Today both main parties, and indeed all three major parties, are attempting to appeal to "the middle ground". There is a use of advertising today to a much greater extent than in the past. It is as if they are trying to sell soap powders, where the difference between brands may be very small. It is not surprising that as well as a period in Conservative Central Office and a period helping other politicians, David Cameron was in public relations. Before that Tony Blair, although he had a period as a barrister, was said by his old headmaster to be above all a good actor. Appearance on the hustings has been replaced by appearance on television.

The membership of the two main parties is a fraction of what it was in the fifties and sixties. The influence of the constituency parties on policy is much less. As Oborne says, our political system today in the age of mass democracy has close resemblances to the oligarchic politics of the 18th century.

Politicians have never been so divorced from ordinary people. The majority of the population would probably agree with the points I have made in this book, but the majority of politicians would, publicly at least, disagree.

What is to be done about this? Firstly we must campaign for victory on the issues I have discussed. Assuming that we are eventually victorious, we need to try and prevent this anomalous situation happening again.

Switzerland goes in for referendums a lot. On a whole number of issues things can only be changed if there is either a simple majority or a two thirds majority in favour of the change. Another possibility is to make experience in the world outside politics or public relations a prerequisite of becoming a member of parliament. There could be an age barrier so that no one could become a minister below a certain age. We could make the selection of a parliamentary candidate to fight a seat the sole prerogative of the constituency party, free from any interference by central office.

All these suggestions might help, but perhaps we should take a closer look at the lives of ordinary members of parliament. Such people have had an interest in politics in their youth and presumably have opinions about various issues. They then work for their chosen political party in the area in which they live and attempt to get selected to fight a winnable seat. The first constituency they will be asked to contest will be an opposition stronghold, but eventually they will be asked to contest a winnable seat and if successful they will become members of parliament. During all this time they will be faithfully following the party line. If they have any ideas of their own they will be putting them aside. Once they are in parliament this behaviour will continue. They will be keen to ingratiate themselves with the party hierarchy. On any particular issue they will be asking themselves not what opinion they have about the matter, but what the party line on it is. If they are lucky they may become junior ministers if their party is in power. If so they will be rewarded for their competence rather than for any deep understanding of the issues in front of them.

The above is a rather cynical but more or less truthful account of what being a member of parliament entails. This situation is regrettable, but it is doubly regrettable when the political class is so divorced from the people it is supposed to represent.

One defect of the existing political set-up is that often ministers are appointed to departments regardless of whether they have any particular knowledge or interest in the issues with which the department deals. Further a minister's stay in a particular department can be severely limited, as he or she can quite often be transferred to another department after a short time. It would be an advantage if a person could continue in the same ministry when his party is in government and in the equivalent post in the shadow cabinet when his party is in opposition.

Most of our politicians have limited experience outside the world of politics. There are virtually none from industry. This could be remedied to some extent if some politicians devoted themselves to specialise in it.

We pride ourselves on our system of government being democratic. It would help if everybody behaved with scrupulous honesty and integrity. These standards would have to be enforced by law or severe public censure, if not their observance would be remarkable rather than constant.

7

Conclusion

In the years immediately succeeding the 2nd World War British politics seemed to revolve around the antagonism between the Labour and Conservative parties. These two represented different constituencies in the country and their members of parliament reflected this. They also had different policies, even though the differences were sometimes more about political attitudes rather than opposing ideas as to what should be done. In spite of their differences, there were a number of things on which almost all members of either party and also almost all members of the public would agree. They would assume that the population of Britain was almost entirely composed of people whose forebears had been there for generations. Furthermore, that it was the job of the freely elected parliament at Westminster and nobody else to enact the laws for the country and govern it. Politicians would assume that the government should first look after the interests of its own people before turning its attention to the rest of the world. There would be an assumption that most companies operating in Britain were British owned and that manufacturing industry was not only desirable, but was the lifeblood of the economy. They would assume that the climate was determined by natural forces over which human beings had no control.

Today all these assumptions of the past have been overturned, not because the majority of the public no longer holds them, but because our political class no longer believes in them. Our political class is no longer composed of people with roots in their particular constituencies, but consists of professional politicians, whose attitudes and ways of life are more similar to each other than to the public whom they purport to represent. The old disagreements about policy have largely disappeared and the political parties are more like rival firms trying to sell their particular brand of soap powder.

In this new situation the old differences between the political parties are irrelevant and the old political allegiances are preserved from force of habit. Before doing anything else we need to embark on the series of policies which I outline below and only after we have completed them can we consider matters of ordinary politics.

Britain should leave the EU.

1) Curb and to an extent reverse immigration.

2) Do everything possible to maintain the union of Britain as one country.

3) Stop overseas aid and engage in trade that is of benefit to both parties.

4) Throw off the stranglehold which the Climatists have over our industry and over our energy production.

5) Go ahead with nuclear energy and shale oil.

6) Control any future takeovers of British companies by foreigners and veto such takeovers of firms deemed to be strategic. Try if possible to recover some of those which have been taken over.

7) Strive to restore utility companies to British control.

8) Revive our education system and expand all technical training.

9) Steadfastly support all high tech research and development.

10) Give full support to British companies.

11) Make sure that in future all those, who are involved in the promotion and protection of British industry and in making decisions affecting it, have had a lifetime of experience in it and are sincerely devoted to ensuring that it prospers.

12) We should realise that free trade was the preferred choice in Victorian Britain, because at that time our country

was the workshop of the world and would benefit from it. Today the situation is entirely different and we need to be more protectionist.

If we do all this, we will, apart from other considerations, be saving ourselves vast amounts of money which we can choose to spend on worthwhile things of our choice, or we can use to reduce the national debt.

In summary we need to eschew the politics of soundbites. Devote ourselves to pursue what is truly worthwhile and make sure that all our policies are made with full consideration of their implications. Let us move forward with boldness and diligence, for ever putting our country above the claims of short term profit.

Corelli Barnett, (1986) *The Audit Of War*, Macmillan London Ltd

Corelli Barnett, (1995) *The Lost Victory*, Macmillan London Ltd

Corelli Barnett, (2011) *The Verdict Of Peace*, Macmillan London Ltd

Gerard Batten, (2012) *Freedom, Security & Justice?*, Caxton Press Ltd

John Besant and Manfred Grunt, (1985) *Management and Manufacturing Innovation in the United Kingdom and West Germany*, Gower Publishing Company Ltd

Phil Blackburn and Richard Sharpe, (1988) *Britain's Industrial Renaissance?*, Routledge

Alex Brummer, (2012) *Britain For Sale*, Random House Group Ltd

Vladimir Bukovsky, (1978) *To Build A Castle*, Andre Deutsch Ltd

Professor S.F. Bush, (2010) *Produce And Prosper*, UKIP Web site (wwww.britain-watch.com/ProduceandProsper)

Garth Clark, (1995) *The Potter's Art*, Phaidon Press Ltd

Nicholas Comfort, (2012) *Surrender*, Biteback Publishing Ltd

Tim Congdon, (2012) *How Much Does The European Union Cost Britain?*, Caxton Press Ltd

Geoff Coyle, (2010) *The Riches Beneath Our Feet*, Oxford University Press

Evan Davis, (2011) *Made In Britain*, Little Brown Book Group

James Delingpole, (2012) *Watermelons*, Biteback Publishing Ltd

Norman Dennis, Fernando Henriques and Clifford Slaughter, (1956) *Coal Is Our Life*, Tavistock Publications Ltd

James Dyson, (2001) *Against The Odds*,Texere LLC

Steve Goreham, (2010) *Climatism*, New Lenox Books

Roger Helmer, (2012) *Keeping The Lights On*, UKIP

Peter Hitchens, (2010) *The Cameron Delusion*, Continuum UK

Bert Hopwood, (1981) *Whatever Happened To The British Motorcycle Industry*, G.T. Foulis & Company

Clare Jenkins and Stephen McClarence, (1989) *On The Knife Edge*, SCL Publishing

Bjorn Lomborg, (2001) *The Sceptical Environmentalist*, Cambridge University Press

Andrew Lorenz, (1989) *A Fighting Chance*, Hutchinson Business Books Ltd

LSE Report, (2010) *The Future Of Finance*, The London School Of Economics and Political Science

Steve Moxon, (2004) *The Great Immigration Scandal*, Imprint Academic

Peter Oborne, (2007) *The Triumph Of The Political Class*, Simon & Schuster

Ian Pilmer, (2009) *Heaven and Earth*, Quartet Books Ltd

John Sergeant, (2005) *Maggie*, Macmillan

S. Fred Singer and Dennis T. Avery, (2008) *Unstoppable Every 1500 Years Global Warming*, Rowman & Littlefield Publishers

Gillian Tett, (2009) *Fool's Gold*, Little Brown Book Group

Richard Vinen, (2009) *Thatcher's Britain*, Simon & Schuster UK Ltd